BEST DAY HIKES IN
Banff National Park

Brian Patton

Best Day Hikes in Banff National Park

Published by
Summerthought

Summerthought Publishing
PO Box 2309
Banff, AB T1L 1C1
Canada
www.summerthought.com

Printing History: 1st Edition – 2019

Text © 2019 by Brian Patton. All rights reserved. No part of this book may be translated, transmitted or reproduced in any form, except brief extracts for the purpose of a review, without prior written permission of the publisher.

Although all reasonable care has been taken to ensure the information in this book is as up to date and accurate as possible, the authors and publisher can accept no responsibility for any loss, injury or inconvenience sustained by any person using the advice contained herein.

All photos © 2019 by Andrew Hempstead, except Kathy Johnson (page 13), Matthew Clay (pages 58, 69, 71, 107), Paul Zizka (page 101 [lower], 145 [lower]), Chuck O'Callaghan (pages 97, 101 [top], 145 [top], 149)
Front cover: Minnestimma Lakes, Larch Valley © 2019 by Paul Zizka/zizka.ca

Design and production: Linda Petras
Printed in Canada by Friesens
Source maps from Natural Resources Canada
(http://open.canada.ca/en/open-government-licence-canada)

We gratefully acknowledge the financial support of the Alberta Foundation for the Arts for our publishing activities.

Library and Archives Canada Cataloguing in Publication

Title: Best day hikes in Banff National Park / Brian Patton & Bart Robinson.

Names: Patton, Brian, author. | Robinson, Bart, author.

Identifiers: Canadiana 20190060948 | ISBN 9781926983394 (softcover)

Subjects: LCSH: Hiking—Alberta—Banff National Park—Guidebooks. | LCSH: Trails—Alberta—Banff

National Park—Guidebooks. | LCSH: Banff National Park (Alta.)—Guidebooks. | LCGFT: Guidebooks.

Classification: LCC GV199.44.C22 B36 2019 | DDC 796.51097123/32—dc23

Contents

INTRODUCTION 4

The Regions 6
Banff's Favourite Hiking Experiences 8
Weather 12
Dangers and Annoyances 14
Planning Your Trip 18

TOWN OF BANFF 26

Tunnel Mountain 28
Hoodoos 31
Spray River Loop 34
Mount Rundle 38
Sulphur Mountain 42
Sundance Canyon 46
Johnson Lake 50
C Level Cirque 53
Lake Minnewanka 56
Stoney Squaw 60
Cascade Amphitheatre 63

BANFF TO LAKE LOUISE 66

Cory Pass 68
Johnston Canyon 72
Rockbound Lake 76
Castle Lookout 80
Sunshine Meadows 84
Rock Isle-Grizzly-Larix Lakes 86
Twin Cairns-Meadow Park 90
Citadel Pass 96
Healy Pass 100
Bourgeau Lake 104
Shadow Lake 108
Arnica Lake 111
Boom Lake 114
Taylor Lake 117

LAKE LOUISE/MORAINE LAKE 120

Lake Agnes 122
Plain of the Six Glaciers 128
Saddleback 132
Paradise Valley 136
Larch Valley 142
Eiffel Lake 146
Consolation Lakes 150

ICEFIELDS PARKWAY 154

Molar Pass 156
Helen Lake 160
Bow Glacier Falls 164
Bow Summit Lookout 168
Chephren Lake 172
Nigel Pass 176
Parker Ridge 180
Wilcox Pass 184

Index 188

About the Author 192

Introduction

With an area of 6,641 square kilometres, Banff is second in size only to Jasper among the mountain parks in the Canadian Rockies. It contains more than 1,500 kilometres of trail, more than any other mountain park, and more day hiking opportunities than all the rest of the parks combined. Since many of these trails are near the park's world-renowned tourist centres of Banff and Lake Louise, they are also among the most heavily traveled in the Canadian Rockies.

Lying on the Alberta side of the Canadian Rockies, Banff protects the entire upper watersheds of the Bow River and North Saskatchewan River, the latter flowing from the Columbia Icefield on its northern boundary. To the east are the foothills, to the west the Continental Divide (which marks the Alberta-British Columbia border), Kootenay National Park, Yoho National Park and Mount Assiniboine Provincial Park. Alberta's Kananaskis Country, which contains a number of provincial parks, including Peter Lougheed Provincial Park, borders the park's southeast. The Canadian Rockies most popular

Rock Isle Lake is a photogenic gem between Banff and Lake Louise.

and scenic drive, the 230-kilometre Icefields Parkway, runs from Lake Louise to the town of Jasper.

Although many of Banff National Park's most spectacular natural landmarks can be admired from the road system, to enjoy the very best of the park, plan on hiking, which is the park's number one draw. Most of the park's short hikes are located near the Town of Banff and at Lake Louise. For those who ride the shuttle bus or gondola, the Sunshine Meadows provide spectacular hiking and a vast variety of wildflowers on the very crest of the Continental Divide. And many longer day hikes radiate from the Icefields Parkway to lakes and alpine meadows between Lake Louise and the Columbia Icefield.

The town of Banff is a good base for exploring the park.

All of the trails detailed in this book are accessed from the park's excellent road system: the Trans-Canada Highway, the Bow Valley Parkway, the Icefields Parkway, Highway 93 South and short access roads leading from the Town of Banff and the village of Lake Louise.

The Town of Banff, the park's main service centre, is located on the Trans-Canada Highway 130 kilometres from Calgary, Alberta and approximately a 90-minute drive from the Calgary International Airport. For information on getting to Banff, read our Planning Your Trip section (page 18).

The Regions

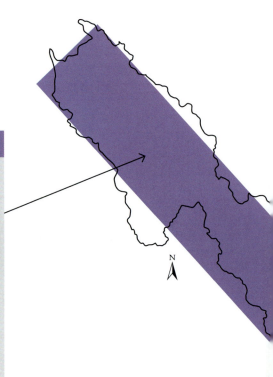

ICEFIELDS PARKWAY

This scenically famous highway winds its way north from Lake Louise to Jasper National Park, with the opportunity to strike out for glacial lakes, remote mountain passes, and colourful wildflower meadows.

LAKE LOUISE/MORAINE LAKE

Two of the park's best known lakes provide the starting point for a great variety of trails. You can hike to historic tea houses, enjoy alpine meadows, and relax beside backcountry lakes.

BANFF TO LAKE LOUISE

From the park's best-known canyon to the famous wildflowers of Sunshine Meadows to high alpine lakes, the hiking trails between Banff and Lake Louise are many and varied.

TOWN OF BANFF

The town of Banff lies in the south of the park, a 90-minute drive west of Calgary. Trails from town rise to surrounding peaks, or explore the lakeshore of Lake Minnewanka or a glacially-carved cirque.

Banff's Favourite Hiking Experiences

JOHNSTON CANYON

The iron catwalks leading through JOHNSTON CANYON (page 72) to a string of waterfalls allow hikers a unique perspective of this natural wonder, but this is also one of the park's busiest trails so plan on an early morning or evening arrival.

SUNSHINE MEADOWS

Straddling the Continental Divide and accessible by gondola or shuttle bus, the wildflower meadows, high alpine lakes, and seemingly endless views from trails such as the Rock Isle-Grizzly-Larix Lakes loop and Citadel Pass make SUNSHINE MEADOWS (page 84) one of Banff's premier day-tripping destinations.

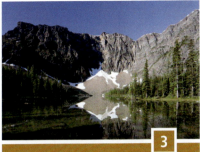

ARNICA LAKE [3]

Named for a yellow flower that thrives around its shoreline, the beautiful setting of **ARNICA LAKE** (page 111) is a just reward for a steep approach. Adding to the charm is the option to extend your day to the Twin Lakes, which are equally stunning—and their solitude offers a real sense of adventure.

LAKE AGNES [4]

High above Lake Louise, **LAKE AGNES** (page 122) is a translucent green body of water surrounded by rugged cliffs, with the option to extend your hike to one of two lofty viewpoints. A lakeside tea house serving hot drinks and homemade goodies only adds to the charm.

PLAIN OF THE SIX GLACIERS [5]

You won't fully escape the crowds of Lake Louise by heading up to the **PLAIN OF THE SIX GLACIERS** (page 128), in the heart of a glacier-clad cirque at the back of Lake Louise, but enjoying tea and home-baked cooking on the verandah of a historic backcountry tea house is still memorable.

INTRODUCTION

BANFF'S FAVOURITE HIKING EXPERIENCES

PARADISE VALLEY — 6

The name says it best. A sparkling creek, an alpine lake, and a photogenic waterfall all surrounded by rugged peaks combine to make **PARADISE VALLEY** (page 136) a wonderful hiking experience in close proximity to Lake Louise.

LARCH VALLEY — 7

Yes, **LARCH VALLEY** (page 142) gets busy, especially in September when the namesake larch are at their golden peak, but strike off early in the morning—preferably very early—and you'll be rewarded with a classic Canadian Rockies combination of subalpine lakes and striking peaks.

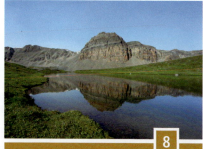

HELEN LAKE — 8

After a short uphill slog through a subalpine forest, the trail to **HELEN LAKE** (page 160) emerges into seemingly endless meadows of wildflowers, followed by alpine tundra inhabited by inquisitive marmots, and finally, the beauty of Helen Lake.

PARKER RIDGE

Short and sweet—**PARKER RIDGE** (page 180) is a great place to experience a true alpine environment with a minimum of effort. The trail up Parker Ridge leads above the treeline to sweeping views across the Saskatchewan Glacier, an arm of the massive Columbia Icefield, and to a string of peaks over 3,000 metres high.

WILCOX PASS

It's outside of Banff's boundary (just), but we've included **WILCOX PASS** (page 184) in this book because the reward-to-effort ratio is hard to beat. In less than 30 minutes of walking, you're presented with panoramic views across to Mount Athabasca and Athabasca Glacier, and the outlook only gets better as you climb higher.

Weather

Despite the northerly latitude of the range, the Canadian Rockies experience climate and weather patterns that compare closely with higher mountain ranges further the south. For example, temperature and annual precipitation in Banff are similar to those of West Yellowstone, Montana, and Leadville, Colorado.

Swimming in glacier-fed lakes is a good way to cool off in summer. Pictured is Chephren Lake.

The hiking season in Banff National Park begins in **SPRING**, usually in early May, when trails in the Bow Valley become snow-free. At this time of year, though, lakes at higher elevations are still frozen and many trails (such as around Lake Louise) are still snow-covered.

The **SUMMER** months of July and August are the prime months to visit, with wildflowers at their peak in late July/early August. In early August, 2018, the town of Banff recorded a temperature of 34.8°C (94.6°F) – the hottest recorded day in the park's history. But even on warm summer days, overnight temperatures can drop to 4°C (39°F) or cooler, so plan accordingly if you are camping.

Temperatures during September, the first month of **FALL**, are distinctly cooler than summer, especially for those camping, when you can expect frost most nights, and even snow. For many visitors, September, when the crowds have

BANFF CLIMATE AVERAGES						
	May	June	July	Aug.	Sept.	Oct.
Maximum temp °C	16°	21°	24°	24°	18°	12°
Minimum temp °C	2°	5°	7°	7°	3°	-1°
Precipitation /mm	50	60	40	50	40	20

gone, is their favourite time to plan a hiking vacation in Banff National Park. By late October, snow has often fallen at higher elevations, although trails around the town of Banff are still enjoyable.

For seven-day weather forecasts in Banff National Park call (403) 762-2088 or go online to weather.gc.ca.

Snow can fall at anytime in the Canadian Rockies. Pictured is Healy Pass photographed in late September after an early fall snowfall.

Dangers and Annoyances

Compared to many of the world's wild regions, Banff National Park is a relatively benign area when it comes to dangerous beasts and other natural hazards. Yet there are a few creatures, both great and small, worthy of discussion.

Bears

While rare, it is a good idea to be prepared for an unexpected bear encounter and, even more importantly, to follow a few basic rules to avoid the encounter in the first place:

- Check trail reports and posted warnings at park visitor centres for a listing of trails where bears have been sighted.
- Watch for bear sign, such as fresh droppings, diggings, or tracks. If you come across an animal carcass, leave the area immediately.

Grizzly bears may be encountered anywhere in the park.

- Always stay alert. You don't want to come upon a bear suddenly at close range. You should continually scan your surroundings, and peruse the slopes and valley ahead before descending from a pass or ridge.
- Make noise in areas where bears have been seen or any prime bear habitat where visibility is limited. The occasional loud shout or whistle will alert bears to your presence. Talking loudly or singing can also be effective.
- Groups of four or more hikers have far less chance of being charged or attacked. Nearly all serious attacks in the park have occurred when a single individual encountered a bear at close range.
- Bear pepper spray has proven effective in driving away aggressive bruins, but for maximum safety each member of the hiking party should be carrying a can and it should be readily accessible.

It is beyond the scope of this book to get into all the variables that must be considered during an encounter with an aggressive bear or a bear attack. Parks Canada publish excellent brochures covering all aspects of avoidance and what to do in an attack situation. Pick one up at a park visitor centre and read it thoroughly.

Other Mammals

Far more people are charged and injured by elk each year than by bears. Aggressive elk are most common around the town of Banff and on nearby trails since these "urbanized" animals have lost their fear of humans. Never

TRAIL RESTRICTIONS

When bears are present, a local closure is put in place for nearby trails. Closures are listed at all visitor centres and closed trails are clearly marked with trailhead signage. In addition to these full closures, seasonal restrictions on the **LAKE MINNEWANKA TRAIL** between mid-July and mid-September require hikers to travel in tight groups of at least four. Similar restrictions are put in place when grizzly bears take up residence in **MORAINE LAKE-PARADISE VALLEY** environs; restrictions when in place apply to **CONSOLATION LAKES, LARCH VALLEY, SENTINEL PASS, EIFFEL LAKE, WENKCHEMNA PASS, SHEOL VALLEY,** and **PARADISE VALLEY**.

While it is usually not too difficult to connect with other hikers to form a group of four at Moraine Lake trailheads, never consider a trip into Paradise Valley unless you organize a group in advance and all members agree to the itinerary.

approach elk at any time of year, but give females with young a very wide berth during the calving season (late May and early June), and the same with bulls during the mating season (late August to early October).

There are no other mammals that pose a significant threat to hikers in Banff National Park. While animals such as cougar and wolverine have fierce reputations, they are usually very shy around humans and very rarely seen.

Of course, there are records of nearly every species having charged or chomped humans at one time or another. (These include an irate mother spruce grouse that permanently scarred the author.) The golden rule around wildlife: always give animals room and never harass or feed them.

Spruce grouse.

Ticks and Other Insects

Wood ticks are abundant in dry, grassy areas of Banff National Park in spring (early May through late June). Although ticks in the Canadian Rockies have been free of Rocky Mountain Spotted Fever and Lyme disease (so far), they can cause a potentially fatal tick paralysis if they burrow at the base of the skull. The best precaution is to wear long pants tucked into socks or gaiters and to avoid lounging about on grassy slopes. Always check your clothing and body carefully following a spring hike. When a tick is discovered, a simple touch or gentle tug often dislodges it. If it has already burrowed into the skin, grasp it as close to the skin as possible with tweezers and pull firmly but slowly. If you can't remove it, or mouthparts remain in the skin, see a doctor.

Mosquitoes are generally less of a problem in Banff National Park than they are in the mountains and wetlands farther north. However, some summers are worse than others and certain areas are renowned for their bloodsucking hordes. Hikers do not need headnets or bug jackets, but repellent should be carried throughout the hiking season until early September.

Horseflies are another common nuisance during midsummer. Insect repellent has no effect on these large biting flies, and a heavy shirt and pants are your only protection.

Giardia

Another addition to the list of hiker miseries is *giardia lamblia*, a waterborne parasite that can cause severe and prolonged gastrointestinal distress. *Giardia* is carried by many species of animals, including humans. While the parasite can find its way into mountain streams and rivers through the feces of many animals, beavers are often blamed, hence the nickname "beaver fever."

Some hikers are willing to take their chances in the upper portions of watersheds, particularly above treeline or where they feel secure there is no beaver activity or human sources of contamination. But the only way to be totally safe is to bring a water purification device or your own bottled water.

Beavers are one of the sources of giardia.

Theft

Vehicle break-ins in Banff National Park are rare but do occur. Vehicles left at remote trailheads, such as those along the Icefields Parkway, are particularly prone. Use common sense and don't leave any valuables in your vehicle. If possible, keep all personal belongings out of sight by leaving them in the trunk. Report break-ins or suspicious behavior to the RCMP in Banff (403/762-2226) or Lake Louise (403/522-3811).

Planning Your Trip

Unless you are simply going for a short stroll, exploring the Banff National Park trail system requires some advance planning. In additional to considering the practical information included in this section, you can use this book to identify which trails suit your abilities and interests in advance of arriving.

While Banff National Park is best known for its natural beauty, the region also offers an excellent tourism infrastructure. Facilities such as accommodations, restaurants, and gas stations are concentrated in the town of Banff and the village of Lake Louise. This allows visitors to spend the day hiking through the wilderness, and then soothe sore muscles in a European-style spa, dine at an upscale restaurant, and rest their heads at a luxurious lodge. For those looking for a simpler experience, campgrounds and hostels are scattered through the park.

Getting to Banff National Park

Primary access to Banff is by highway: the **TRANS-CANADA HIGHWAY** from the east and west, the **ICEFIELDS PARKWAY** from the north (Jasper), and **HIGHWAY 93 SOUTH** from southeastern British Columbia via Radium and Kootenay National Park. Calgary lies 130 kilometres to the east and Vancouver 845 kilometres to the west, both via the Trans-Canada Highway. Highway 93 serves as a direct link north from the United States via Cranbrook, British Columbia. The town of Jasper is linked to Banff National Park by the Icefields Parkway. It's 287 kilometres between the towns of Jasper and Banff.

Getting Around Banff National Park

The closest airport handling domestic and international flights is in Calgary, a 1.5-hour drive to the east. Airporter buses run on a regular schedule to and from Banff.

All major car rental companies have outlets at the Calgary International Airport and in the town of Banff, but reservations should be made well in advance. You will need a vehicle to access trailheads away from the town of Banff and

Renting an RV or camper is a good way to experience Banff National Park.

Roam Transit buses are easily recognized by the wildlife images that adorn them.

Lake Louise/Moraine Lake centres. Another option is an RV or camper rental, and these should also be made well in advance.

ROAM TRANSIT (roamtransit.com) is a public transit bus system that provides an inexpensive way to return by bus after walking the Hoodoos trail and also to access trails along the Lake Minnewanka Road. Roam buses also link Banff and Lake Louise, with an additional summer route via the Bow Valley Parkway and Johnston Canyon. **PARKS CANADA SHUTTLES** operate between late May and early October throughout the Lake Louise region, with departures from the Lake Louise Park & Ride, along the Trans-Canada Highway southeast of the village. For more information, visit the Parks Canada webpage: pc.gc.ca/banffnow.

Trailhead Parking

Our advice is simple—arrive early to be assured of a parking spot at most trailheads, especially those at Lake Minnewanka, Johnston Canyon, Lake Louise, and Moraine Lake. To be assured of a spot at Lake Louise or Moraine

Shuttle buses depart from the Lake Louise Park & Ride to ease traffic congestion at the lake.

Camping is an inexpensive way to enjoy the Canadian Rockies.

Lake, plan on arriving before 8am—and preferably before 7am. When the parking lot at Moraine Lake is full (usually before 7am), the road is closed and no traffic is allowed on Moraine Lake Road.

When the parking lots at Lake Louise and Moraine Lake are full, visitors will be directed to the Lake Louise Park & Ride, eight kilometres (five miles) southeast of the village along the Trans-Canada Highway, from where shuttle buses to the two lakes depart regularly.

Visit the Parks Canada webpage: pc.gc.ca/banffnow for up-to-date traffic and parking status throughout the park, Lake Louise and Moraine Lake shuttle information, and downloadable PDFs such as *Public Transit Banff National Park*.

Campgrounds

Most campgrounds in Banff National Park begin opening in mid-June, and all but Tunnel Mountain are closed by late September. All campsites have a picnic table and fire ring (firewood is supplied for an additional charge). Sites in the most popular campgrounds (Tunnel Mountain, Two Jack Lakeside, Johnston Canyon, and Lake Louise) can be reserved through the **PARKS CANADA CAMPGROUND RESERVATION SERVICE** (877/737-3783, reservation.pc.gc.ca) starting in early January. If you're travelling June through September, and know which dates you'll be in Banff, it is strongly advised to take advantage of this service.

On most nights in summer, and especially on summer weekends, every campsite in every campground in Banff National Park fills, often by lunchtime.

Information

Official park visitor centres are located at Banff and in Lake Louise.

Once you've arrived, the best place to make your first stop is the **BANFF VISITOR CENTRE** (224 Banff Ave., open mid-May to early Oct. 8am-8pm, and early Oct. to mid-May daily 9am-5pm). This downtown complex houses information desks for **PARKS CANADA** (403/762-1550, pc.gc.ca/banff) and **BANFF & LAKE LOUISE TOURISM** (403/762-0270, banfflakelouise.com), as well as a small retail shop selling books, maps, and bear spray.

The **LAKE LOUISE VISITOR CENTRE** (201 Village Road, 403/522-3833, open daily 9am-5pm and extended hours of daily 8:30am-7pm June to Sept.) is beside Samson Mall in the village of Lake Louise.

> **TRIP PLANNING WEBSITE**
>
> One of the advantages of the digital age is the ability to provide important information immediately so you can plan your Banff hiking adventure. That's why we've created the website CANADIANROCKIESTRAILGUIDE.COM, which contains a wide array of information designed to supplement this book. The website includes: **TRAIL UPDATES**, so you can go online and check to see if there have been any changes or disruptions to your route; a **HIKING BLOG**, which includes personal hiking reports, seasonal news, Parks Canada policy updates, and gear recommendations; **HIKING EBOOKS** that focus on specific areas of interest, such as family hikes and waterfalls; and **RESOURCES** such as webcams, weather forecasts, and trip planning information.

If you are heading south from Jasper into Banff, stop at the **GLACIER DISCOVERY CENTRE**, opposite the Columbia Icefield along the Icefields Parkway. Parks Canada operates an information desk inside the centre (780/852-6288, 10am-5pm daily early May-late Sept.), where you can pick up brochures and learn about trail conditions in the immediate area.

The website canadianrockiestrailguide.com is dedicated to Canadian Rockies hiking. It includes a hiking blog by the authors of this book, trail updates, digital downloads, and a wide range of hiking resources.

Maps

While the maps in this book cover each of the trails described, they are only designed to give you a general idea of trail location, course, and surrounding topography. It's always nice to have a more detailed map along to identify natural features and to help dispel confusion. **GEM TREK** produces the *Banff Up Close* (1:35,000) and *Best of Lake Louise* (1:35,000) maps showing all hikes around the town of Banff and Lake Louise. Other Gem Trek maps cover nearly all the popular day hikes in this book and include *Banff-Egypt Lake* (1:50,000), *Lake Louise & Yoho* (1:50,000), *Banff & Mount Assiniboine* (1:100,000), *Bow Lake & Saskatchewan Crossing* (1:70,000), and *Columbia Icefield* (1:75,000). Gem Trek maps (gemtrek.com) are sold at Park Visitor Centres and many retail outlets throughout Banff National Park.

What to Pack

Even if you're planning a short walk, it is essential that you are prepared for changing weather. While the following recommendations will help you decide what to pack, the lighter you travel the more enjoyable your time in the wilderness will be.

While hikers can walk many of these trails in running shoes, you should always have sturdy walking shoes or hiking boots available to cope with muddy, rocky and rooty tracks. If you have a new pair of shoes or boots, wear them once or twice before leaving home—just to make sure they are comfortable.

In summer, temperatures rarely drop below freezing, but you should prepare for a variety of weather conditions (especially if visiting in spring and fall) by dressing in layers. The best clothing is made from synthetic fabrics, which draw perspiration away from the body yet repel water. A breathable rain jacket should be carried regardless of the weather forecast. We always carry a warm hat (toque) and gloves throughout the year as insurance, but they are always necessary for longer hikes in spring and fall.

Trekking poles significantly reduce stress on knees, especially on steep descents. They also decrease strain on feet and lower backs. While ski poles are better than nothing, serious hikers will want to invest in purpose-built telescopic, anti-shock, lightweight poles with flexible tips.

While natural sunlight is good for our health, too much can have adverse effects. This is especially relevant at higher elevations, where the air is thinner and cleaner, and the effects of UV exposure more pronounced. Always apply sunscreen, bring sunglasses, and some sort of sun hat.

How very Canadian! These hikers crossing the Brazeau River made trekking poles by cutting down hockey sticks.

> ### TRAIL ETHICS
>
> **STAY ON THE TRAIL**, even if it means muddy boots. Leaving the trail creates parallel tracks and widens existing trails. Shortcutting switchbacks causes erosion.
>
> **LEAVE ROCKS, FLOWERS, ANTLERS, AND OTHER NATURAL OBJECTS UNDISTURBED**. Never pick wildflowers or other plants.
>
> **NEVER FEED, DISTURB, OR HARASS WILDLIFE**. It is illegal, harmful to the animal's health, and alters their natural behaviour.
>
> **PACK OUT ALL GARBAGE**. Carry plastic bags and, whenever possible, pack out litter that other, less considerate hikers have left behind.
>
> **USE WASHROOM FACILITIES PROVIDED AT MOST TRAILHEADS**.
>
> **GIVE HORSEBACK PARTIES THE RIGHT-OF-WAY**. If you encounter a horseback party, step well off the trail and stand still until it has passed.

It is essential to stay hydrated when hiking, especially at higher elevations. Due to the possible presence of *giardia* (see page 17), use water purification devices or bring bottled water.

The day hikes detailed in this book do not require any special dietary considerations, although on longer walks it is important to keep your energy level up by eating high-octane carbohydrates, such as those found in energy bars. Remember to pack all garbage out. Do not leave anything behind—even apple cores.

Bug spray is a summer necessity. You can pick up the brands that are most effective at outdoor retailers and convenience stores throughout Banff National Park. A pre-packaged first aid kit can come in handy for longer hikes, but is not necessary for short walks. Even if you don't carry a complete kit, blister moleskin (available at most drugstores) or band-aids should be carried at all times. A spare plastic bag is handy for packing out garbage.

Carry everything in a lightweight daypack. The best daypacks are durable but lightweight, have padded shoulder straps and back panel, and are waterproof or come with a rolled up waterproof pack cover built into the base. Waterproof stuff sacks provide extra defense on rainy days.

Town of Banff and Vicinity

Most park visitors base themselves in the town of Banff, a bustling community of 9,000 permanent residents located a 90-minute drive west of Calgary with a choice of accommodations and five campgrounds within close proximity. Nestled in a forested valley, the town is surrounded by hiking trails—leading along rivers and ascending the surrounding mountains. Nearby are opportunities for visitors to walk back through history, explore a variety of lakes, and climb to a glacially-carved cirque.

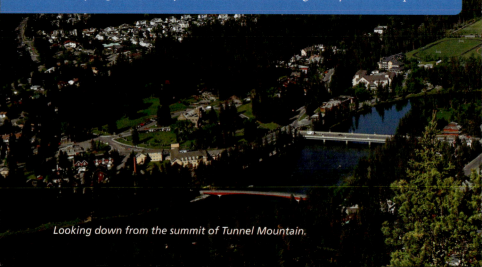

Looking down from the summit of Tunnel Mountain.

Tunnel Mountain

The Tunnel Mountain hike is short and readily accessible from downtown Banff. The summit offers excellent views of the Banff environs, the north ridge of Mount Rundle, and a 30-kilometre stretch of the Bow Valley. It is one of the oldest trails in the park and a popular outing for Banff residents.

Length: 2.3 km (1.4 miles) one way
Elevation gain: 260 metres (845 feet)
Allow: 45 minutes one way
Rating: Easy/moderate
Map: Gem Trek *Banff Up Close*

Trailhead N51°10.523′ W115°33.708′

Drive or walk from downtown Banff on Wolf St. to St. Julien Road. Stay right and follow St. Julien uphill for 300 metres to the trailhead parking area, located on the left side of this ascending street.

Trail Outline

- **0.0** Trailhead (elevation 1,430 metres).
  —Steady climb through forest.
- **0.4** Trail crosses Tunnel Mountain Drive.
- **1.7** Summit ridge switchback. Viewpoint.
- **2.3** Tunnel Mountain summit (elevation 1,690 metres).

Trail Description

A series of sweeping switchbacks make a gradual but steady ascent through a thick forest of lodgepole pine and Douglas fir. Once you cross the Tunnel Mountain Drive (an optional starting point if you want to shorten your hike), there are occasional glimpses of the town and valley. These openings culminate at a good viewpoint beside a series of limestone slabs near the summit ridge—a panorama that includes the town and the Fairmont Banff Springs. A few rare limber pines grow beside the trail.

On the summit ridge, the trail doubles back and climbs gradually above the mountain's sheer, east-facing cliffs. Views along the ridge extend over the Banff Springs Golf Course and down-valley to the park's eastern boundary near Canmore.

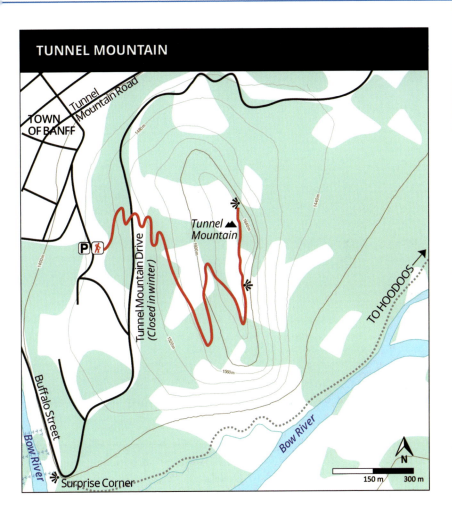

The trail ends on the sparsely-forested summit, which was once the site of a fire lookout tower (1941-1977). Limestone outcrops just west of the summit provide the best views up the Bow Valley to the west and include Banff, the Vermilion Lakes and Massive Range. (Look for crinoid, coral and brachiopod fossils in the limestone slabs.)

Views from the top of Tunnel Mountain extend west across the town to the Bow Valley and the distant Massive Range.

Hoodoos

You can reach the Hoodoos by road from Tunnel Mountain Road, or take a more interesting approach to these intriguing geological formations by hiking beneath Tunnel Mountain from Surprise Corner. The hiking route is particularly rewarding in June and July, when meadows are filled with the blooms of blue flax, harebells, and brown-eyed Susans.

Length: 4.7 km (3 miles) one way
Elevation gain: 90 m (300 feet)
Allow: 1.5 hours one way
Rating: Easy/moderate
Map: Gem Trek *Banff Up Close*

Trailhead N51°10.027' W115°33.539'

Follow Buffalo Street southeast from Banff Avenue for 1.2 km to a small parking area at Surprise Corner. The trail begins on old stone stairs leading down into the forest.

Trail Outline

- **0.0** Trailhead (elevation 1,435 metres).
  —Descend stone stairs and veer left.
- **1.2** Trail emerges at Bow River (elevation 1,375 metres).
- **1.6** Bow River splits, trail continues through open forest.
- **2.5** Junction. Continue straight ahead.
- **3.5** Tunnel Mountain Road.
  —Trail parallels road.
- **4.3** Hoodoos Viewpoint parking area.
- **4.7** Hoodoos Viewpoint (elevation 1,465 metres).

Trail Description

From Surprise Corner viewpoint, the trail descends old stone stairs and veers sharply left, descending gradually through the forest to the Bow River. From this point, it follows beneath the towering cliffs that form Tunnel Mountain's east face. After 1.6 kilometres, the river

Elk are commonly seen along the Hoodoos Trail.

splits and the trail follows the bank of the west channel through an open forest where elk often graze. Soon you are climbing through open stands of aspen, lodgepole pine and Douglas fir to Tunnel Mountain Road. From this point, the trail parallels the road the rest of the way to the Hoodoos Viewpoint parking area. A variety of viewpoints with interpretive displays are spread along the final 1.2-kilometre stretch of trail.

The Hoodoos are weirdly shaped pillars rising from a steep ridge overlooking the Bow River. They are carved from the glacial till that composes the ridge. As the ridge eroded, some of the rock, gravel and sand was cemented by the soil's high lime content and became resistant to weathering. The result is consolidated material standing in the form of pillars.

> **OPTION**
>
> While you can complete a circuit of Tunnel Mountain by walking back to town along the road, you can also catch a **ROAM TRANSIT BUS** that services the nearby campgrounds throughout the summer.

Looking across the Hoodoos to Mount Rundle.

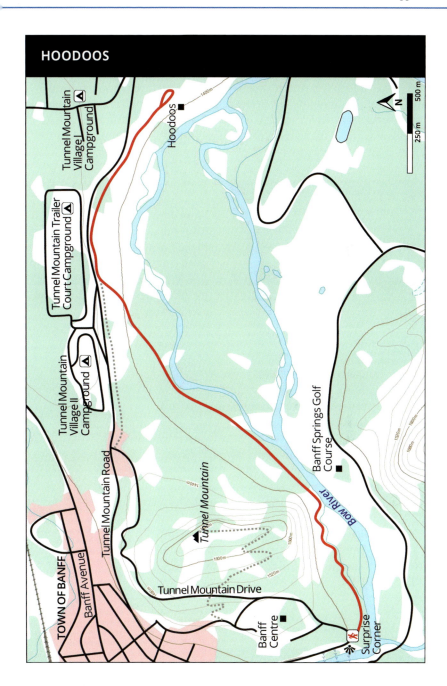

Spray River Loop

This popular loop trip runs up one side of the Spray River and back down the other from a trailhead just beyond the Fairmont Banff Springs. Though it follows abandoned fire roads most of the way, it is a pleasant outing that is seldom far from the river—a favourite trip for cyclists in summer and cross-country skiers in winter.

Length: 10.7 km (6.6 miles) roundtrip
Elevation gain: 75 metres (250 feet)
Allow: 3-4 hours roundtrip
Rating: Easy/moderate
Map: Gem Trek *Banff Up Close*

Trailhead N51°09.644′ W115°33.565′

From downtown Banff, cross the Bow River bridge and follow Spray Avenue to the Fairmont Banff Springs. Follow around a traffic circle and beneath a pedestrian overpass, continuing for 200 metres to the trailhead parking area.

Trail Outline

- **0.0** Trailhead (elevation 1,415 metres).
- **0.7** Junction. Spray River west side trail ahead.
  —Turn left for Spray River and east side trail.
- **0.9** Spray River footbridge and picnic area (elevation 1,360 metres).
  —Cross bridge and turn right to follow trail upstream.
- **1.5** Junction. Golf course and Old Quarry Loop left. Spray River Loop right.
- **5.0** Mount Rundle Campground.
- **5.8** Spray River footbridge.
- **5.9** Junction and cleared area with trail shelter (elevation 1,435 metres). Goat Creek ahead.
  —Turn right for Spray River west side return.
- **7.0** Junction. Banff Gondola left (3.0 km). Stay ahead.
- **10.0** Junction (loop split). Stay straight ahead.
- **10.7** Trailhead (elevation 1,415 metres).

Trail Description

From the trailhead parking area, follow the broad track of the old Spray River Fire Road south into the forest. When you reach a junction at 0.7 km, you have a choice. Skiers and cyclists will likely prefer to continue straight ahead on the broad track and complete the circuit counterclockwise. But if we're hiking, we like to do it clockwise by branching left and descending to a footbridge over the Spray River (nice views downstream to the Fairmont Banff Springs and Mount Norquay).

Cross the bridge and continue upstream beneath slabs of the old Rundle Rock quarry then climb steeply to a junction

Looking downstream to the Fairmont Banff Springs from the footbridge 900 metres from the trailhead.

This bridge across the Spray River is the turnaround point.

with the Spray River east side trail. Now you're back on broad track and can continue up-valley to the far end of the circuit, where a bridge crosses to the west side trail and a pleasant, open area by the river.

Complete your outing by turning downstream and following the gently rolling, 4.8-kilometre track above the Spray River back to the trailhead.

The final section of trail follows an old fire road along the west side of the river.

OPTION

The 4.3-kilometre **OLD QUARRY LOOP** is a shorter circuit from the Spray Avenue trailhead. Hike the Spray River Loop to the 1.5-kilometre junction then turn left and follow the east side trail north towards the golf course, from where you have an elevated view of the Spray River far below. Stay left at all junctions to return upstream to the Spray River footbridge. Cross back over and retrace your steps to the trailhead. The namesake quarry (pictured), where the bridge crosses to the east side of the river, was the source of Rundlestone used on the exterior of the Fairmont Banff Springs.

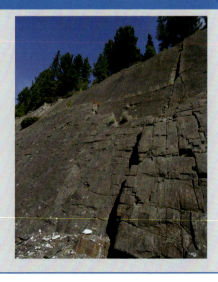

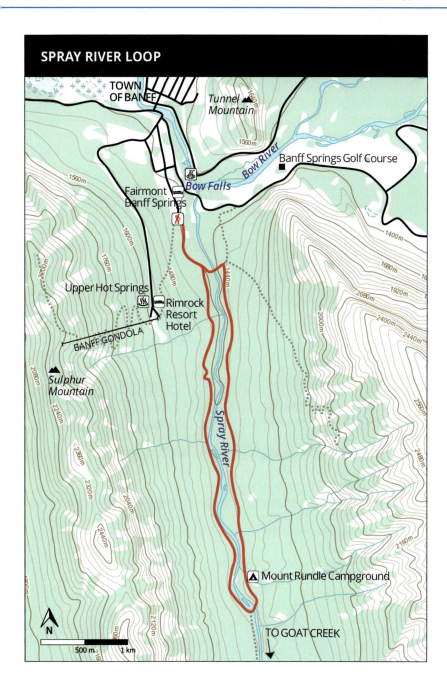

Mount Rundle

The trail up the southwest slope of Mount Rundle is steep and mostly enclosed by forest. While it does offer occasional views of the Spray Valley, its primary function is as an approach route to the mountain's 2,949-metre summit—the most popular climb in Banff National Park.

Length: 4.7 km (2.9 miles) one way
Elevation gain: 470 m (1,550 feet)
Allow: 1.5-2 hours one way
Rating: Moderate
Map: Gem Trek *Banff Up Close*

Trailhead N51°09.906' W115°33.183'

From downtown Banff, cross the Bow River bridge and turn left onto Spray Ave. Continue on Spray Ave. 800 metres to Bow Falls Ave. Turn left and follow it downhill to the Bow Falls. Park here and walk along the golf course access road across the Spray River bridge. Follow this paved road 400 metres to the trailhead (signed) in the forest on the right side of the roadway.

Trail Outline

- **0.0** Trailhead (elevation 1,360 metres).
  —Trail skirts behind golf course green.
- **0.2** Junction. Stay left.
- **1.0** Junction. Mount Rundle trail branches left from the Spray River Loop.
  —Trail climbs through pine forest.
- **3.8** Spray Valley viewpoint.
- **4.7** Trail's end (elevation 1,830 metres). Route to main peak of Mount Rundle continues across major gully.

The first expansive valley views are enjoyed at the 3.8-kilometre mark.

Trail Description

The Mount Rundle trail strikes off from the golf course access road just beyond the first green on the right, skirts behind it and, at a junction, branches left on a broad track leading up into the forest. This old access road climbs well above the Spray River on its ascent along the east side of the valley as the Spray River Loop.

Just 800 metres beyond the golf course, the Mount Rundle trail branches left from the Spray River Loop and begins its steady climb up the mountain's southwest slope. You are enclosed by forest for the first three kilometres. The trail then switchbacks onto open slopes and there are good views of the Spray Valley.

The hiking trail contours along the slope in a southeast direction until it eventually ends at the edge of a major gully, which is unofficially known as Central Gully. Looking up this gully, you can see the limestone slabs and talus slopes leading to the top of the mountain.

OPTION

The climb to the **SUMMIT OF MOUNT RUNDLE** can be made by fit scramblers, but the peak lies a gruelling 1,120 metres above the official end of the trail. The correct route follows across the gully and up the ridge on the opposite side (ascending the gully itself leads to serious problems). Anyone continuing beyond the official end of the hiking trail should pick up a copy of the pamphlet *A Scrambler's Guide to Mount Rundle* at the Park Visitor Centre in Banff, or download it from the Parks Canada website. The trail and the mountain slopes beyond are bone dry, so be sure to carry water on the hike or the climb.

Central Gully marks the official end of the trail.

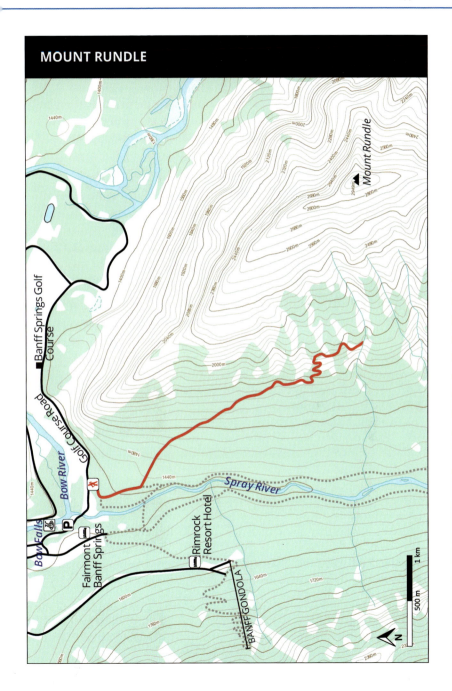

Sulphur Mountain

For those who disdain using a gondola lift to reach a mountaintop, the 5.5-kilometres trail from the Upper Hot Springs is the preferred route to the summit ridge of Sulphur Mountain. While the trail gains nearly 700 metres from bottom to top, 28 switchbacks keep the grade reasonable and ease the strain of the ascent.

Length: 5.5 km (3.4 miles) one way
Elevation gain: 680 metres (2,215 feet)
Allow: 2 hours one way
Rating: Moderate/difficult
Map: Gem Trek *Banff Up Close*

Trailhead N51°08.971' W115°33.564'

Follow Mountain Drive from downtown Banff 3.5 km to its termination at the Upper Hot Springs parking lot. The trailhead is signposted near the entrance to the parking area.

Trail Outline

- **0.0** Trailhead (elevation 1,580 metres).
  —Follow broad uphill trail. Steady switchbacks.
- **2.4** Trail passes within 200 metres of waterfall.
- **2.7** Old trail shelter site.
  —Switchbacks beneath gondola line.
- **5.5** Banff Gondola Summit (elevation 2,260 metres).

Trail Description

The track is wide and grades are moderate as the trail climbs the heavily-forested east slope of Sulphur Mountain, though views do open briefly as it passes just north of a waterfall. At km 2.7, a short side trail branches right to the site of an old trail shelter (removed in 2002). Prior to the completion of the gondola in 1959, a tractor and wagon transported visitors up the trail to this point, which is the halfway point on the hike.

The grade is steeper near the summit as you switchback back and forth beneath the gondola line.

Passing under the gondola as the trail nears the summit.

A scattering of alpine larch in the forest heralds your arrival at the 2,260-metre summit ridge and the busy Banff Gondola Summit with its interpretive displays, gift shop and much-needed refreshments.

And once you get to the top, if you don't really want to hike back down the trail, you can ride the gondola down in eight minutes flat! (One-way tickets are only available for the downhill ride and must be purchased at the gondola ticket office in advance.)

The view from Sulphur Mountain. Tunnel Mountain can be seen in the centre of this photo, with Cascade Mountain on the left and Lake Minnewanka in the distance.

OPTION

No hike up Sulphur Mountain would be complete without continuing north along the Sulphur Mountain Boardwalk to a promontory known as **SANSON PEAK**, where views of the town of Banff, the Bow Valley and Lake Minnewanka are even more expansive than from the Banff Gondola Summit. The route follows what is most certainly the most lavish alpine trail in Canada—a 600-metre boardwalk, complete with viewing platforms, that leads to a stone weather observatory constructed in 1903. (The 2,270-metre peak is named for park meteorologist Norman Sanson, who hiked up the mountain over 1,000 times until his retirement in 1931.)

Weather observatory on Sanson Peak.

When you are immediately beneath Sanson Peak, you'll see an abandoned road leading down the mountain to the left. This road once serviced the Cosmic Ray Station, constructed at this junction on the ridge as part of Canada's contribution to the 1957-58 International Geophysical Year. This laboratory studied the bombardment of the earth's atmosphere by high-energy galactic particles until 1978. The building and its equipment were removed in 1981.

45

SULPHUR MOUNTAIN

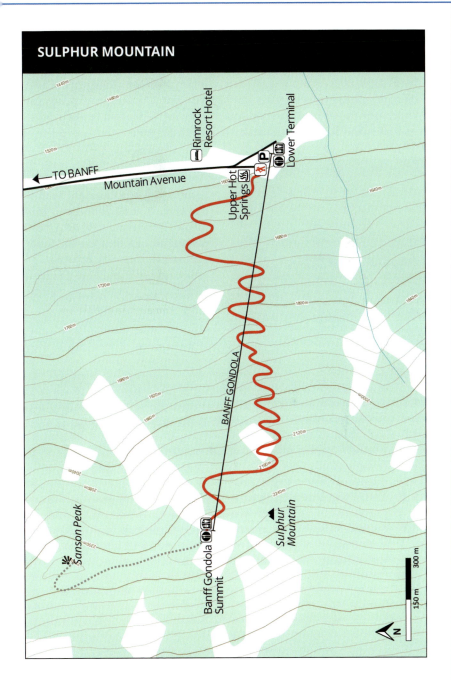

Sundance Canyon

This pleasant little canyon was once accessible by road from the town of Banff. Today, the road beyond the Cave and Basin is a paved walking and cycling path. While many people bike to the canyon, the first half of the trail boasts open views along the Bow River and makes a fine evening walk.

Length: 4.3 km (2.7 miles) one way
Elevation gain: 155 metres (510 feet)
Allow: 1 hour one way
Rating: Easy
Map: Gem Trek *Banff Up Close*

Trailhead N51°10.118′ W115°35.683′

From the intersection at the south end of the Bow River bridge in Banff, follow Cave Avenue 1.2 km to the parking area for the Cave and Basin National Historic Site. A paved walkway leads to the Cave and Basin complex and continues 200 metres beyond to the trailhead kiosk.

Trail Outline

- **0.0** Trailhead (elevation 1,410 metres).
  —Gradual descent into forest on broad paved trail.
- **0.7** Junction (elevation 1390 metres). Marsh Loop right.
  —Flat walking beside Bow River.
- **1.8** Trail climbs into forest.
- **2.2** Junction. Sulphur Mountain left; Brewster Creek and Sunshine Road right.
- **3.1** Sundance Canyon Picnic Area.
- **3.3** End of paved trail. Bike stands.
  —Follow foot trail into Sundance Canyon.
- **4.3** Sundance Canyon summit (elevation 1,545 metres).
  —Trail loops back to paved trail, from where it's 3.3 km back to the trailhead.

47

The first stretch of trail is paved, and follows the Bow River for a short stretch.

Trail Description

From the trail kiosk beyond the Cave and Basin complex, the trail descends gradually through forest to the Bow River. For the next 1.5 kilometres it follows along the river and its side channels with views of the rugged peaks to the north, including the sharp spire of Mount Edith. (The experience is tempered somewhat by the scent of a well-used horse trail that follows beside the pavement.)

The final stretch to the canyon climbs

Water flowing out of Sundance Canyon.

TOWN OF BANFF AND VICINITY

SUNDANCE CANYON

gradually through forest. You pass a junction where an old access road leads to the summit of Sulphur Mountain (left 5.6 kilometres) and Brewster Creek (right). But you'll continue ahead and follow the paved trail until it passes the Sundance Canyon Picnic Area and ends just beyond. A foot trail continues into the canyon proper (no bikes are permitted beyond the pavement).

When you reach the canyon, you can follow the original Sundance Canyon loop trail, a 2.1-kilometre circuit that climbs beside Sundance Creek for one kilometre before circling right through dense forest and descending back to the end of the paved trail. In addition to the canyon with its mini-cascades, you pass a viewpoint for the Massive Range at the 1.4-kilometre mark of the loop, but the vista is more obscured by trees than when the trail was constructed many decades ago.

Biking is a good way to reach Sundance Canyon.

OPTION

The 1.6-kilometre **MARSH LOOP** circling the Cave and Basin marsh is a popular nature walk that provides an alternate view of the unique, warm-spring wetland. You can hike it as a short nature walk from the Sundance Canyon trailhead, or if you're returning from Sundance Canyon, it makes an interesting way to end your trip. If returning from Sundance Canyon, leave the paved trail where it heads uphill, away from the Bow River, and follow a broad, dirt path downstream beside the river. You soon emerge on the north side of the marsh, looking back across to the viewing platforms and the Cave and Basin complex. There are often signs of beaver and muskrat activity along this shoreline, and waterfowl on both the river and marsh can be easily identified with binoculars. At the east end of the marsh, turn right and cross an earthen dike back to the Cave and Basin parking area.

Marsh Loop.

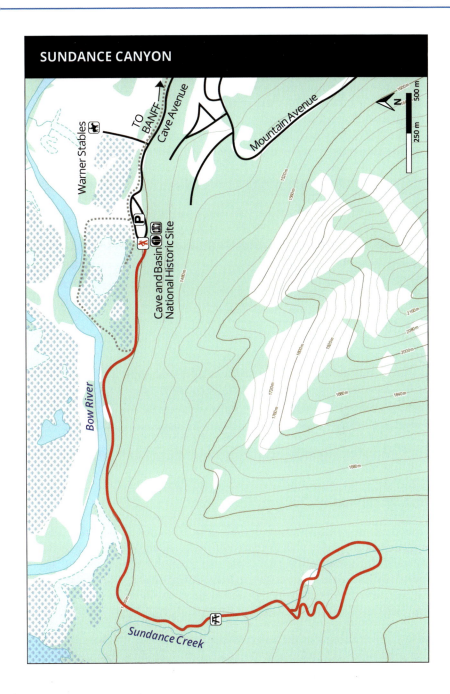

Johnson Lake

The trail around Johnson Lake is a fine early season walk, often snow-free by late April. The hike provides variety throughout the hiking season, including montane wildflowers, loons, and nesting waterfowl. By hiking around the lake counter-clockwise, you will enjoy continuous views of Mount Rundle and Cascade Mountain as you return along the north shore.

Length: 3 km (1.9 mile) one way
Elevation gain: none
Allow: 45 minutes roundtrip
Rating: Easy
Map: Gem Trek *Banff Up Close*

Trailhead N51°11.966' W115°29.377'

Follow the Lake Minnewanka and Johnson Lake roads 6.8 km from the Trans-Canada Highway interchange to Johnson Lake picnic area.

Trail Outline

- **0.0** Trailhead (elevation 1,416 metres).
  —Walk downhill to outlet bridge at lake's west end.
- **1.0** Junction. Unsigned path to abandoned cabin.
- **1.4** Cross dike at east end of lake.
- **2.6** Inlet creek bridge.
- **2.8** Junction. Picnic area bypass to parking area right. Picnic area trailhead left.
- **3.0** Picnic area trailhead.

Trail Description

From the Johnson Lake parking lot, walk downhill across a small earth-fill dam and bridge, then angle uphill to a powerline. After a brief run beneath the wires, the trail branches left into the forest and rolls along above the lake's south shore (purple calypso orchids flower here in May). Approximately one kilometre into the hike, scan the woods to the right for an old cabin—home to Billy Carver, "the Hermit of Inglismaldie," between 1910 and the mid-1930s.

At the far end of the lake, the trail crosses an earthen dike, where you get your first good views back to Cascade Mountain. Returning along the north shore,

JOHNSON LAKE

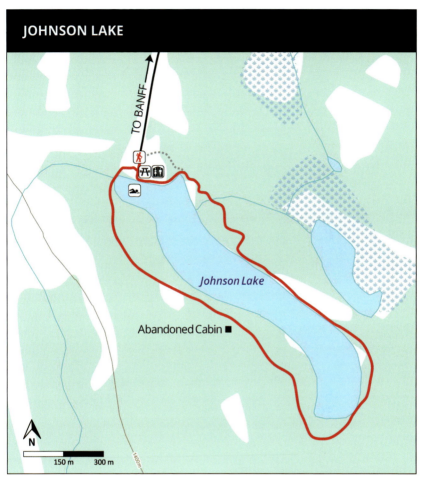

you cross grassy slopes which are filled with the yellow blooms of brown-eyed Susan (*gaillardia*) in July, and skirt the margins of a dry Douglas fir forest. There are pockets of burned trees, remains of the Fairholme prescribed burn (2003), and some wonderful, old aspen groves as you complete the circuit back to the picnic area.

Early mornings are your best chance to see and hear loons at Johnson Lake.

Looking over Johnson Lake to Mount Rundle.

C Level Cirque

The C Level Cirque trail is one of the more attractive hikes in the Banff-Lake Minnewanka vicinity. In less than four kilometres it climbs past artifacts of the long-defunct Bankhead coal operation and a panoramic viewpoint for Lake Minnewanka to a high, rockbound pocket beneath the sheer east face of Cascade Mountain.

Length: 3.9 km (2.4 miles) one way
Elevation gain: 455 metres (1,500 feet)
Allow: 1.5 hours one way
Rating: Moderate
Map: Gem Trek *Banff Up Close*

Trailhead N51°14.209′ W115°31.194′

From the Trans-Canada Highway at the Banff East Exit interchange, follow Lake Minnewanka Road 3.5 km to Upper Bankhead Picnic Area. The trail begins at the far (west) end of the picnic area parking lot.

Trail Outline

- **0.0** Trailhead (elevation 1,465 metres).
  —Steady uphill through forest.
- **1.1** Old mine building and viewpoint (100-metre spur).
- **1.8** Mine shaft vent holes.
- **3.9** C Level Cirque (elevation 1,920 metres).

Trail Description

The trail begins its ascent through a pleasantly varied forest of lodgepole pine, aspen and spruce, where calypso orchids, blue clematis and many colourful violets bloom in early summer.

Within a half-hour you reach a skeletal building, the remnants of an anthracite coal operation that flourished in the area from 1904 to 1922. A town of nearly

Mine buildings along the C Level Cirque trail.

C-LEVEL CIRQUE

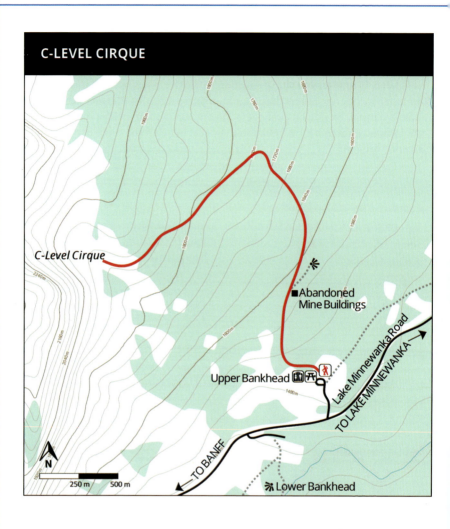

1,000 inhabitants called Bankhead was spread across the valley where the trail begins, and these old buildings were a part of the "C Level" operation—the highest coal seams worked within the eastern slope of Cascade Mountain.

From behind the cement transformer building, follow a faint, overgrown trail through scrub trees 100 metres to a ridge of coal tailings that provides an excellent view out to Lake Minnewanka. The Palliser Range stretches away from the northern shoreline, while Mount Inglismaldie (2,965 metres) and the

Fairholme Range rise above the lake's southern shores. Both ranges were the site of prescribed fires set in the early 1990s through 2003.

Back on the main trail, you climb above the C-Level buildings and viewpoint and soon pass by several fenced holes, which were once air vents for the mineshafts below. The rest of the hike is a steady climb through forest until, 200 metres before reaching the cirque, views open down the Bow Valley to Mount Rundle, the Three Sisters and other mountains beyond the town of Canmore.

"Cirque" is a French word used by geologists to describe a semicircular, bowl-shaped depression created by an alpine glacier, and C Level Cirque is a miniature example of the phenomenon. Though the glacier that produced the basin has long since disappeared, snow often lingers in the basin into midsummer. As it retreats, a carpet of yellow glacier lilies spreads across the damp, subalpine soil near its entrance. A tiny pond below the trail provides water throughout the summer, fed by the extensive snowfield on the talus slopes above.

From the rockslide at the edge of the cirque, a faint trail continues up to the right along a sparsely-forested ridge to an even higher vantage point above the basin. However, most hikers prefer to "boot ski" the snowfield beneath Cascade's cliffs or simply relax on a convenient rock to watch the antics of the local inhabitants—hoary marmots, pikas and golden-mantled ground squirrels.

Another local resident in spring is the wood tick, so no lounging in the grass! And be sure to check your body and clothes carefully following early season outings.

The final destination is C Level Cirque.

Lake Minnewanka

The trail along the north shore of Banff's largest lake is attractive to early and late season visitors since its low elevation and location in the Front Ranges usually provides dry, snow-free hiking from May until mid-autumn. Mountain bikes are also permitted along the entire length of the trail, so expect their company if you hike here.

Length: 7.8 km (4.9 miles) one way
Elevation gain: 45 metres (150 feet)
Allow: 2 hours one way
Rating: Easy/moderate
Map: Gem Trek *Banff Up Close*

Trailhead N51°14.902' W115°29.850'

From the Trans-Canada Highway, follow the Lake Minnewanka Road 5.5 km to the parking area at Lake Minnewanka. The trailhead is the access gate just before the concession.

Trail Outline

- **0.0** Trailhead (elevation 1,480 metres).
  —Trail follows old paved road around picnic area.
- **0.4** Small rocky cove.
- **0.6** End of paved road, trail information board.
- **1.4** Stewart Canyon bridge.
- **1.5** Junction. Stay right.
- **3.0** Lake Minnewanka viewpoint (elevation 1,525 metres).
  —Trail rolls east above lakeshore.
- **7.8** Aylmer Lookout Junction.

Trail Description

From the boat dock and picnic area at the west end of Lake Minnewanka, a paved road passes behind a large day use area and emerges at a rocky cove with a driftwood-strewn beach. After passing a covered picnic shelter, the paved road ends at a trail sign and narrows before entering a forest. Beyond this point, the trail climbs slightly for good lake views before reaching Stewart Canyon, a worthwhile destination in itself for the high footbridge spanning the narrow chasm.

Stewart Canyon.

Beyond the canyon, the trail climbs over a low, forested ridge, then rolls along the north shore of Lake Minnewanka with little gain or loss of elevation. Whether you hike or bike, you will enjoy many views of the lake and the Fairholme Range beyond.

Burned forest along sections of the route dates between 1988 and 2003 when Parks Canada set prescribed burns to emulate the valley's prehistoric fire regime.

The landscape becomes noticeably drier as you continue east and the vegetation more typically montane. Limber pine is scattered among the stands of lodgepole, and western wood lilies, brown-eyed Susans, flax, harebells and other dry-land wildflowers cover grassy hillsides in early summer.

Lake Minnewanka is always close by on this trail.

Although the trail along Lake Minnewanka continues beyond the 7.8-kilometre mark, this spot is a good turnaround point for those looking for a half-day hike. Read below for two options to extend your hike.

NOTE: Due to bear activity, travel on Lake Minnewanka trail is restricted to groups of at least four people hiking in close proximity from July 15 until September 30. Check with the Banff Visitor Centre or website for alterations to this policy.

OPTIONS

The trail beyond the 7.8-kilometre junction continues along the lakeshore for over 20 kilometres to DEVIL'S GAP at the far end of the lake. Scenery is similar to the first section, although there will be less foot and bike traffic.

At our recommended turnaround point, 7.8 kilometres from the trailhead, a trail forks left to AYLMER LOOKOUT. From this junction, it is another four kilometres and 560 metres of vertical to reach the old lookout site and its panoramic view of Lake Minnewanka. Hiking to the lookout and back adds 2.5-3 hours to your day, but many strong hikers feel it's worth it. Away from the tranquility of the lake begins a strenuous climb indeed, gaining nearly 300 metres of elevation over the next two kilometres. Since this slope is usually snow-free in early June, and one of the hot spots in the Canadian Rockies on sunny days, you should carry an adequate supply of water to complete the ascent. The site of the defunct Aylmer fire lookout is on the end of an open ridge

Aylmer Lookout.

below the summit of Mount Aylmer. After labouring up the steep draw leading toward Aylmer Pass for 45 minutes or more, watch for the lookout trail branching right. The trail to the lookout continues steeply upwards from this junction, angling southeast towards the crest of the ridge. Nearly all of Lake Minnewanka can be seen from this 2,040-metre viewpoint. The water, over 500 metres below, is of the deepest blue, and boats look like tiny water insects skimming to-and-fro. Across the lake, the twin summits of Mount Inglismaldie and Mount Girouard arise, displaying massive cliffs of Mississippian and Devonian-age limestone. (Wood ticks are common here in spring, so check your body and clothes carefully upon returning from this trip.)

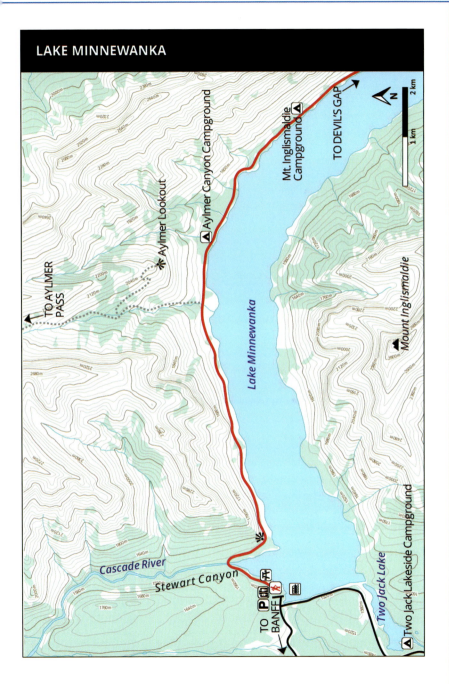

Stoney Squaw

Like Tunnel Mountain, across the valley, Stoney Squaw is not really a mountain, just an 1,884-metre promontory extending east from the slopes of Mount Norquay. It is one of the highest, easily reached viewpoints overlooking the town of Banff and the Bow Valley.

Length: 2.1 km (1.3 miles) one way
Elevation gain: 185 metres (570 feet)
Allow: 45 minutes one way
Rating: Easy/moderate
Map: Gem Trek *Banff Up Close*

Trailhead N51°12.040′ W115°35.714′

From the Trans-Canada Highway at the Banff West Exit, follow the Mount Norquay Road north six km to the Mount Norquay ski area. Turn right into the main parking lot and watch for the trail sign just inside the entrance to the right.

Trail Outline

- **0.0** Trailhead (elevation 1,700 metres).
  —Steady climb through forest.
- **1.9** Views south to Banff and the Bow Valley.
- **2.1** Stoney Squaw summit (elevation 1,884 metres).

Trail Description

This moderately graded but steady uphill trail is enclosed in a dense forest of lodgepole pine and spruce most of the way, but as you near the top you begin to catch glimpses of the Banff environs. The Bow Valley and the town of Banff lie immediately below, and Tunnel Mountain, Mount Rundle, and Sulphur Mountain are all visible beyond.

Views at the largely treed summit are limited, though you do have a fine, close-up of the rugged south face of Cascade Mountain, the distinctive pyramid peak that most visitors only view at a distance from Banff Avenue. And there are more extensive views down the Bow Valley to the park's eastern boundary and Canmore.

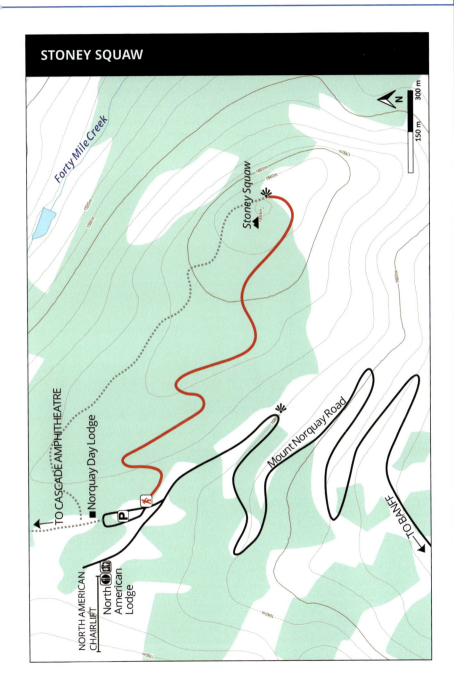

OPTION

You can make a slightly-longer loop back to the trailhead by descending northwest from the summit on a faint path that soon turns into good trail. This track descends through a dense, mossy forest on the cool **NORTH SIDE OF STONEY SQUAW**. When you reach the top of a clearing, walk down the slope to the ski area service road, turn left and follow it to the day lodge, main parking lot, and trailhead.

The view of Cascade Mountain from Stoney Squaw summit.

Cascade Amphitheatre

One of the longer and more strenuous day trips near the town of Banff leads up the western flank of Cascade Mountain to a natural amphitheatre. This hanging valley, enclosed by the limestone cliffs of the mountain's summit ridges, features lush subalpine wildflower meadows and immense rockslides inhabited by marmots and pikas.

Length: 7.7 km (4.8 miles) one way
Elevation gain: 640 metres (2,100 feet)
Allow: 2 to 2.5 hours one way
Rating: Moderate/difficult
Map: Gem Trek *Banff Up Close*

Trailhead N51°12.190′ W115°35.880′

Follow Mount Norquay Road north from the Trans-Canada Highway six km to the Mount Norquay ski area. Enter the first parking lot on the right and park in front of the day lodge.

Trail Outline

- **0.0** Trailhead (elevation 1,700 metres).
  —Descend through lodge complex on ski-area service road.
- **0.6** Spirit Chairlift. Forty Mile Creek trail left. Enter forest to right.
- **1.0** Trail emerges at base of Mystic Chairlift.
- **3.1** Forty Mile Creek bridge (elevation 1,555 metres).
- **4.3** Junction. Elk Lake trail ahead. Cascade Amphitheatre right.
- **6.6** Amphitheatre entrance. Gradual uphill through meadows.
- **7.7** Amphitheatre headwall (elevation 2,195 metres).

Trail Description

The Cascade Amphitheatre hike begins at the Mount Norquay ski area's day lodge. Continue through the lodge plaza and straight down-valley on the main service road. The first one kilometre can be a bit confusing as you work your way past the base stations of a number of ski lifts, but stay on the service road and ignore branch trails into the forest on the right. After 600 metres, the trail up Forty Mile Creek to Mystic Pass branches left. Stay right and enter the forest behind the Spirit Chairlift. After a few hundred metres, the trail emerges at the base of the Mystic Chair, then reenters the forest and broad trail begins.

After a steady descent through lush, flower-filled forest, the trail reaches Forty Mile Creek, turns right and crosses the creek on a substantial bridge. Just beyond the bridge, the forest opens to a view of the sheer 390-metre-high face of Mount Louis—one of the most demanding rock climbs in the Canadian Rockies. The rugged summit of Mount Edith, another popular climb, can be seen south of Louis and behind Mount Norquay.

The last trail fork on the trip appears 1.2 kilometres beyond the Forty Mile Creek bridge, where the Amphitheatre trail branches uphill to the right from the Elk Lake trail. A relentless series of switchbacks transport you upwards through a dense forest of spruce and lodgepole pine for 2.3 kilometres to the cool, subalpine forest at the mouth of the Cascade Amphitheatre.

From the amphitheatre entrance, the trail extends for just over one kilometre to a headwall created by the mountain's main summit ridge. The moist meadows along the way are carpeted with wildflowers throughout much of the summer, beginning with white-flowered western anemone and nodding yellow glacier lilies along the edges of receding snow banks in late June. Two small sink lakes also appear in the meadows with the spring snowmelt, but these usually disappear by early July. Rockslides enclosing the upper end of the cirque are home to hoary marmots and pikas as well as the occasional white-tailed ptarmigan.

A narrow trail winds its way through Cascade Amphitheatre.

While the ascent of Cascade Mountain from the amphitheatre is not particularly difficult, the route is tricky and can be dangerous at certain times of the year. If you want to go for the summit, pick-up a copy of *A Scrambler's Guide to Cascade Mountain* at the Park Visitor Centre in Banff.

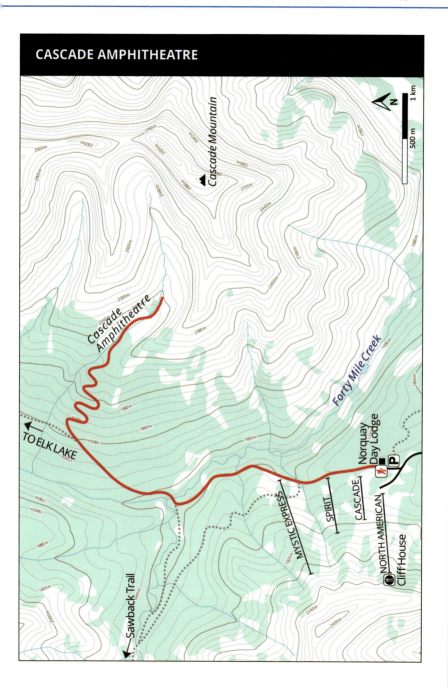

Monarch Viewpoint, Sunshine Meadows.

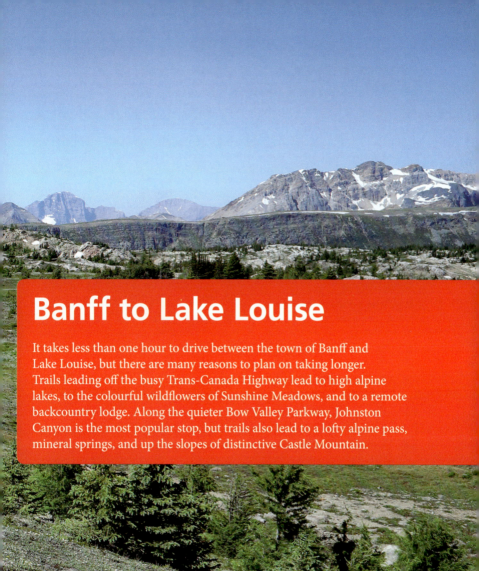

Banff to Lake Louise

It takes less than one hour to drive between the town of Banff and Lake Louise, but there are many reasons to plan on taking longer. Trails leading off the busy Trans-Canada Highway lead to high alpine lakes, to the colourful wildflowers of Sunshine Meadows, and to a remote backcountry lodge. Along the quieter Bow Valley Parkway, Johnston Canyon is the most popular stop, but trails also lead to a lofty alpine pass, mineral springs, and up the slopes of distinctive Castle Mountain.

Cory Pass

Cory Pass is the highest and most spectacular hike near the town of Banff. The 2,350-metre-high gap frames the monolithic south face of Mount Louis to create a view that is usually reserved for mountaineers. And after gaining almost a vertical kilometre in elevation to get there, you will feel like a mountaineer.

Length: 5.8 km (3.6 miles) one way
Elevation gain: 915 metres (3,000 feet)
Allow: 2.5 hours one way
Rating: Difficult
Map: Gem Trek *Banff Up Close*

Trailhead N51°10.443′ W115°39.267′

Follow the Bow Valley Parkway northwest from the Trans-Canada Highway for 300 metres. Turn right and drive one km to the Fireside Picnic Area. The trailhead is across the bridge.

Trail Outline

- **0.0** Trailhead (elevation 1,435 metres).
- **1.1** Junction. Edith Pass trail ahead. Cory Pass uphill to left.
- **1.7** Cory Knoll viewpoint.
- **2.4** Crest of narrow forested ridge.
- **5.8** Cory Pass (2,350 metres).

Trail Description

From the Fireside Picnic Area, the trail runs through coniferous forest and pleasant aspen groves to a junction at kilometre 1.1. Turn left and begin a heart-pounding climb up an open, south-facing slope. After a brief rest on a grassy knoll overlooking the Bow Valley, continue steeply upward to a forested ridge and the first views of Cory Pass.

Climb along this rocky, sparsely forested ridge for another one kilometre or so to the top of a small cliff band (an easy down-climb through an obvious break in the rock). The trail picks up again at the base of this cliff, soon emerges from the trees, and climbs across an open slope to the pass (take care if snow is lingering in the steep gullies crossed by the trail).

Situated at 2,358 metres between the rugged cliffs of Mounts Edith and Cory, Cory Pass is often a very cold, windy place. However, the views are worth any discomforts, especially north beyond the pass to the grey limestone slabs of Mount Louis—one of the most difficult rock climbs in Banff National Park (it was first climbed by Conrad Kain and Albert McCarthy in 1916).

NOTE: Do not underestimate the physical exertion that this hike requires. The trail is also hazardous when the ground is frozen or there is snow and ice on sections of the route.

Fall colours along the first section of the trail to Cory Pass.

The view east to Mount Louis from Cory Pass.

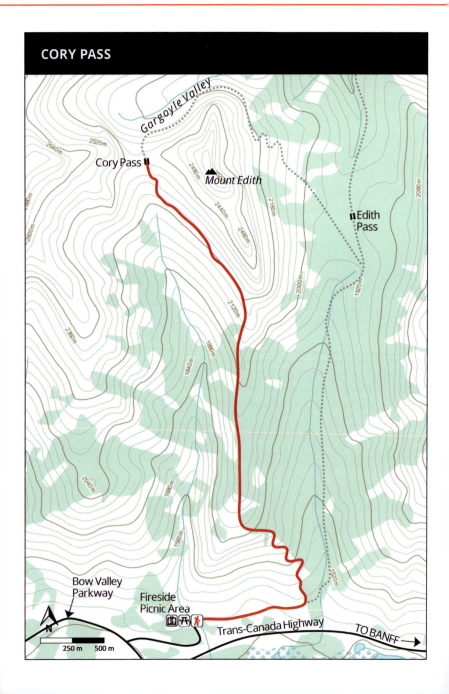

OPTION

The gargoyles of Gargoyle Valley.

Instead of going back the way you came, you can descend the north side of the pass and make a loop around Mount Edith via the Edith Pass trail.

Barring lingering snow in early summer, a vague trail leads down steep talus and into **GARGOYLE VALLEY**, named for the rock pinnacles just north of the summit. After a quick loss of elevation, a rocky but defined track traverses right beneath Mount Edith's cliffs and just above the floor of the valley—an incredible, rock-filled sanctuary dominated by Mount Louis's imposing south face.

Rocky trail leads through the mouth of the Gargoyle Valley to an open rockslide and a view of the broad Forty Mile Creek Valley. Hikers sometimes lose the trail here, so look for the long scree slope leading up to the right. A faint trail climbs directly up this rocky slope for approximately 300 metres and, near the top, branches left off the scree and into stunted trees.

The trail traverses lightly-forested slopes beneath Mount Edith and eventually plunges down the mountainside on an avalanche slope, re-enters the forest, and intersects the main Edith Pass trail 600 metres south of its summit. Turn right and follow this trail down through mossy-floored forest and back to the 1.1-kilometre junction with the Cory Pass trail.

Total distance for the loop is 13 kilometres, and taking into account the steep climbs and descents, it makes for a very strenuous day. Whether you simply hike to the pass and return or complete the loop around Mount Edith, you are in for a good workout. Do not underestimate the physical exertion that this hike requires. The trail is also hazardous when the ground is frozen or there is snow and ice on sections of the route.

Johnston Canyon

Every day throughout the summer, hundreds of visitors follow canyon-clinging catwalks and cliff-mounting staircases to Johnston Canyon's Lower and Upper Falls. While the canyon and its unique trail are certainly worthy of a visit, you'll have to do the hike in the evening or very early in the morning to avoid the crowds.

Length: 2.7 km (1.7 miles) to Upper Falls
Elevation gain: 135 metres (445 feet)
Allow: 45 minutes one way
Rating: Easy
Map: Gem Trek
Banff & Mount Assiniboine

Trailhead N51°14.815′ W115°50.445′

Follow the Bow Valley Parkway northwest from the Trans-Canada Highway 17.5 km to Johnston Canyon. The parking area is on the east side of Johnston Creek. Follow the trail across a footbridge to Johnston Canyon Resort and trailhead.

Trail Outline

- **0.0** Trailhead (elevation 1,430 metres).
  —Gradual climb into canyon.
- **1.1** Lower Falls.
- **1.9** Twin Falls.
- **2.3** Stella Falls.
- **2.5** Marguerite Falls.
- **2.7** Upper Falls (elevation 1,565 metres).

Trail Description

The trail begins immediately behind the main building at Johnston Canyon Resort. After a short climb through the forest, it descends and stays close to Johnston Creek all the way to Lower Falls. Along the way you pass over sturdy iron catwalks attached beneath overhanging canyon walls, where the turbulent waters of the creek flow beneath your feet.

At **LOWER FALLS** there is a bridge across the creek, which serves as a viewpoint for the thundering cataract. A short tunnel through the canyon bedrock allows

These iron catwalks lead through Johnston Canyon.

passage to an even more intimate vantage point (often spray-soaked).

Back on the main trail, you continue up the canyon via more catwalks and broad, well-graded trail. There are viewpoints overlooking the canyon and Twin Falls (1.9 km), Stella Falls (2.3 km), and Marguerite Falls (2.5 km). The latter two waterfalls are named for family members associated with Johnston Canyon Resort, which started as a tea house in 1913. The original trail to the Upper Falls was built by Walter Camp in the early 1930s, at which time he named one of the falls enroute for his wife, Marguerite.

Lower Falls.

Along the trail beyond the Lower Falls, scan the creek and its banks for dippers. Also known as water ouzels, these solitary, slate-grey birds are often seen bouncing up and down on streamside rocks.

At the 30-metre-high **UPPER FALLS**, there are two viewpoints: the bottom of the falls is reached by a side-trail and catwalk leading to a viewing platform; a short steep climb on the main trail takes you to the top of the falls and another viewing platform, which hangs out over the gorge above the waterfall.

OPTION

A small percentage of hikers continue beyond the Upper Falls three kilometres to the **INK POTS**, a natural phenomena where seven cold mineral springs bubble to the surface in open meadows beside Johnston Creek. The high point of the trail is reached a short way beyond the Upper Falls, from where it's a steady downhill walk to open meadows at the Ink Pots, located on the right side of the trail not far from the creek. While the Ink Pots are unique (they have a constant temperature of 4°C/39°F and their basins are composed of quicksand), the wild setting, open, willow meadows of the Johnston Creek Valley and views of the Sawback Range are the main reward. Allow 1.5 hours to reach the Ink Pots from the Johnston Canyon Trailhead.

Ink Pots.

JOHNSTON CANYON

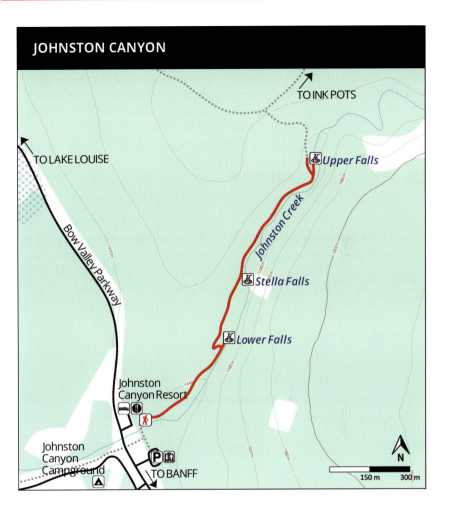

NOTES: While the rock slabs near the brink of the falls are fenced, people still clamber through to be near the creek. Be forewarned: if you slip into the stream, you will be swept over the falls! (Always stay on the trail and keep children under control.)

The trail up Johnston Canyon is one of the busiest in the park. Early morning or evening is a good time to plan a hike, especially in July and August. When the main parking lot is full, plan on parking in the overflow lot along the Johnston Canyon Campground access road.

Rockbound Lake

This rigorous hike leads to two distinctly different lakes beneath the massive cliffs of Castle Mountain. Tower Lake is a placid, green mirror fringed by open subalpine forest and lush wildflower meadows; Rockbound Lake is a cold, grey sheet contained by tumbled boulder-fields. Both lakes are overshadowed by the impressive Eisenhower Tower and the limestone cliffs of Castle Mountain.

Length: 8.4 km (5.2 miles) one way
Elevation gain: 760 metres (2,50 feet)
Allow: 2.5 to 3 hours one way
Rating: Moderate/difficult
Map: Gem Trek
   Banff & Mount Assiniboine

Trailhead N51°16.142′ W115°54.948′

Follow the Bow Valley Parkway to Castle Junction, 30 km northwest of the town of Banff. The paved parking area for the trail is on the north side of the Parkway 200 metres southeast of Castle Mountain Chalets.

Trail Outline

- **0.0** Trailhead (elevation 1,450 metres).
- **0.3** Silverton Falls junction.
- **5.0** Wide track narrows. Steady climb into subalpine meadows.
- **7.7** Tower Lake.
- **8.4** Rockbound Lake (elevation 2,210 metres).

Trail Description

The Rockbound Lake trail starts on an old access road, which provides little scenic interest as it climbs gradually along the southern flank of Castle Mountain. Eventually it gains sufficient elevation to provide glimpses of the Bow Valley and the mountains to the west. Prominent are pyramid-shaped Copper Mountain and, to the south, Pilot Mountain, which served as a landmark to Canadian Pacific Railway (CPR) surveyors charting the line of the railway down the valley in 1881. The trail, still following the old roadbed, continues its traverse around the end of Castle Mountain and finally enters the high valley running northwest between its ramparts and Helena Ridge.

After five kilometres the trail narrows to a single track and, just a bit farther on, views open to the Eisenhower Tower on Castle Mountain, a 2,752-metre-high limestone pinnacle rising in front of the main body of the mountain. The trail beyond this point can be rather messy, particularly early in the season when the entire area is soggy from the melting snow.

An extensive meadow leads to **TOWER LAKE**, a small body of water set within a semicircle of rock. This appears to be the end of the journey, but the trail continues to the right of the lake and climbs steeply up the headwall beyond.

At the top of the cliff you catch your first view of Rockbound Lake and immediately appreciate the aptness of the name. It is totally enclosed by rock. Cathedral Formation limestone contains the bed of the lake, while Stephen and Eldon Formation limestone creates the high walls of the cirque. The lake lies precisely in the centre of a major down-fold in the strata—the Castle Mountain Syncline, which starts here and runs all the way to Mount Kerkeslin in Jasper National Park, some 260 kilometres to the northwest.

From the scattered forest of Engelmann spruce, alpine fir and larch at the top of the headwall, you can explore the Rockbound basin: huge boulders beyond

Tower Lake.

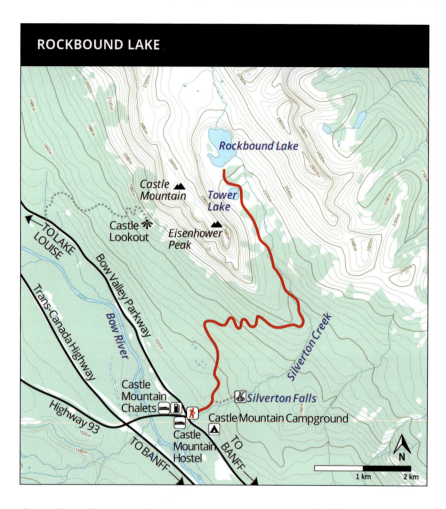

ROCKBOUND LAKE

the southern shore provide a playground for novice rock climbers, and the slopes of Helena Ridge to the east are easily ascended for a better perspective of the amphitheatre.

Rockbound Lake.

OPTION

Though the impressive 50-metre-high **SILVERTON FALLS** is a short 900-metre hike from the Bow Valley Parkway, it is a natural feature few people know about or visit. The creek and falls are named for the nearby mining town of Silver City (Silverton was a name proposed for the town), which boomed briefly in 1883-84 then disappeared.

The hike starts on the Rockbound Lake trail and branches right from that route after 300 metres. Another 600 metres through dense forest brings you to a viewpoint near the top of the falls. Total elevation gain for the trip is only 90 metres.

Silverton Falls.

Castle Lookout

This short, steep trail up the slopes of Castle Mountain leads to the site of an abandoned fire lookout and an excellent panorama of the Bow Valley stretching from the grey limestone peaks near the town of Banff to the glacier-capped summits near Lake Louise.

Length: 3.8 km (2.4 miles) one way
Elevation gain: 550 metres (1,800 feet)
Allow: 1.5 hours one way
Rating: Moderate
Map: Gem Trek
 Banff & Mount Assiniboine

Trailhead N51°17.611′ W115°58.468′

Follow the Bow Valley Parkway 4.8 km northwest from Castle Junction to the trailhead parking area—set back in the forest on the north side of the road.

Trail Outline

- **0.0** Trailhead (elevation 1,460 metres).
- **1.5** Old cabin.
- **2.2** Trail narrows. Broad trail narrows to single track.
 —Moderate to steep switchbacks.
- **3.8** Castle Lookout (elevation 2,010 metres).

Trail Description

Since the Castle Lookout trail climbs along a slope with a southwesterly exposure, it is one of the earliest trails at this elevation to be free of snow in the spring (early to mid-May) and one of the latest to remain snowfree in autumn.

From the parking area, follow a steep, wide pathway upward through forest of lodgepole pine, spruce and occasional Douglas fir. The dense forest allows only a few glimpses of the Bow Valley over the first two kilometres, but the remains of a log cabin offer a stop of interest (the collapsed structure possibly dates to the short-lived mining boom in this part of the valley circa 1884).

The broad trail eventually reverts to single-track 700 metres beyond the cabin and traverses out onto the steep, sparsely forested slopes overlooking

Looking northwest toward Mount Temple from the trail.

the Bow Valley. In early summer this open forest produces a colourful array of wildflowers, including Indian paintbrush, columbine, and heart-leaved arnica.

As you gain elevation, views up and down the Bow Valley improve. Finally the trail twists up through a cliff band, enters a stand of whitebark pine, and contours to the right above the precipice for 100 metres to the old lookout site.

All that remains at the site is the foundation of the lookout cabin, which was constructed by labourers from the park's conscientious objector camps in the autumn of 1942. It was abandoned

The remains of this log cabin lie right beside the trail.

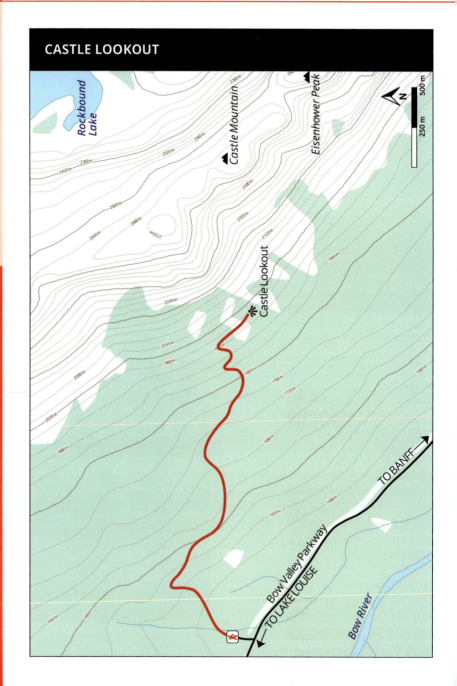

by Parks Canada in the mid-1970s and accidentally burned by visiting hikers in 1983.

This open ridge provides views to most of the major peaks overlooking the Bow Valley. Most prominent down valley is Pilot Mountain, to the southeast. Directly across the valley to the south is 3,161-metre Storm Mountain. Beside Storm is the broad gap of Vermilion Pass, which contains Highway 93 South, known as the Banff-Windermere Highway when it was opened as the first public road into southeastern British Columbia in 1923. One of the most distinctive peaks from this vantage point is the ice-and-snowcapped Mount Temple (3,544 metres) to the northwest, rising between Moraine Lake and Lake Louise as the third highest summit in Banff National Park.

When you're finished taking in the view, check yourself over closely for wood ticks after any spring trip to the lookout.

The view from Castle Lookout. The peak right of centre is Storm Mountain.

SUNSHINE MEADOWS

The Sunshine Meadows region is unique in the Canadian Rockies. Unlike most of the Continental Divide, which is composed of glaciated peaks and towering limestone and quartzite walls, the 15-kilometre stretch of the divide between Citadel Pass and Monarch Ramparts is a mixture of subalpine and alpine meadowland. Pacific weather systems flowing in from the west add their moisture to create a vast, rolling rock garden with an incredible variety of wildflowers, some of which appear nowhere else in the range.

In the centre of this exceptional landscape is **SUNSHINE VILLAGE**—a lofty 2,200-metre starting point for three major hikes leading into Sunshine Meadows. These hikes are detailed on the following pages, including the Rock Isle-Grizzly-Larix Lakes Loop, Twin Cairns-Meadow Park, and Citadel Pass.

All trails in the region are well marked.

Getting to Sunshine Village

Unlike all other hiking trails detailed in this book, Sunshine Meadows is not accessible by road. Instead, access during the hiking season is by **GONDOLA** or **SHUTTLE BUS**. A five-kilometre long gondola that serves skiers throughout the winter provides access from the Bourgeau Base Area to Sunshine Village from July to August Friday through Monday. A shuttle bus provides access from the gondola base to Sunshine Village July to August Tuesday through Thursday and daily for the first three weeks of September.

To get to the Bourgeau Base Area, follow the Trans-Canada Highway to the Sunshine Village interchange, nine kilometres west of the town of Banff. Continue on the Sunshine Road for another nine kilometres to the parking area at the gondola base station. You can also hike the six-kilometre service road from the gondola base station, but it is a long, dismal approach (bikes are not permitted).

Sunshine Mountain Lodge.

Once up at the village, you can ride the Standish Chairlift (fare included with gondola/shuttle bus tickets) to elevate you even closer to the meadows.

Sunshine Village

Visitors to Sunshine Meadows begin their adventure by taking the gondola or shuttle bus to Sunshine Village, which sits at a lofty elevation of 2,200 metres. In the village, Centennial Lodge contains interpretive displays, a retail outlet, and a cafe. During foul weather, this building is a welcome refuge, while on a warm afternoon the deck is a pleasant place to relax at day's end while awaiting the shuttle. Also in the village is Trapper's Pub, also with a pleasant deck, and **SUNSHINE MOUNTAIN LODGE** (sunshinemountainlodge.com), providing comfortable overnight accommodations, a café, and a restaurant.

For complete information, schedules and rates for the gondola, chairlift and shuttle bus, log onto banffsunshinemeadows.com.

Rock Isle-Grizzly-Larix Lakes

The trail to Rock Isle, Grizzly and Larix Lakes is the most popular half-day outing in the Sunshine Meadows region. It includes extensive wildflower meadows and, as a bonus, a viewpoint at Rock Isle Lake that is one of the most photogenic scenes in all of the Canadian Rockies.

Length: 8.5 km (5.3 miles) roundtrip
Elevation gain: 105 metres (350 feet)
Allow: 2.5 to 3 hours roundtrip
Rating: Easy/moderate
Map: Gem Trek
   Banff & Mount Assiniboine

Trailhead N51°04.712′ W115°46.942′

For information on getting to Sunshine Village, see page 84. From Sunshine Village, continue above the day lodge on a gravel roadbed following the trail to Rock Isle Lake.

Trail Outline

- **0.0** Trailhead (elevation 2,200 metres).
—Follow gravel road uphill.
- **1.2** Continental Divide (elevation 2,305 metres). Alberta-B.C. boundary.
- **1.3** Junction. Citadel Pass left. Rock Isle Lake-Grizzly-Larix Lakes ahead.
- **1.8** Rock Isle Lake Viewpoint.
- **2.0** Junction. Grizzly-Larix Lakes left. Twin Cairns-Meadow Park right.
- **2.9** Junction. Trail split for Grizzly-Larix Lakes loop. Keep right.
- **3.4** Grizzly Lake.
- **4.4** Simpson Valley Viewpoint.
- **4.6** Larix Lake.
- **5.4** Junction. Return to trail split at 2.9 km.
- **8.5** Trailhead (elevation 2,200 metres).

Trail Description

Following a broad gravel track from the centre of Sunshine Village, you make a steady but brief climb to the Continental Divide, passing through the last scattered stands of alpine fir into a treeless alpine landscape. (Columbian ground squirrels will greet you as you climb, bounding through fields of tall,

Rock Isle Lake is one of the most photogenic scenes in the Canadian Rockies.

fuzzy western anemones gone-to-seed.) On the 2,305-metre summit, views stretch south across the vast Sunshine Meadows to the distant pyramid of Mount Assiniboine.

West of the divide, you enter British Columbia and Mount Assiniboine Provincial Park, passing the Citadel Pass trail junction and descending to Rock Isle Lake Viewpoint. In the early morning, the waters of Rock Isle Lake are often a mirror reflecting its rocky island and shoreline. There is a peacefulness and natural symmetry in the scene, including distant peaks in British Columbia that has attracted artists and photographers for many decades.

From the Rock Isle Lake Viewpoint, the trail veers to the west and quickly reaches the junction for the Twin Cairns-Meadow Park trail. Stay left. The trail climbs over a low, rocky hill to where the lake's outlet stream plunges down steep limestone slabs. From this wonderful natural waterslide, you see across the Simpson Valley to the distant peaks of Kootenay National Park.

Continuing beyond the lake's outlet, the trail drops through open forest and lush meadows filled with wildflowers. Soon the trail splits to begin a

Larix Lake.

2.5-kilometre loop around Grizzly and Larix Lakes. Keep right and descend to Grizzly Lake, where scarring from a 2017 wildfire can be seen on the distant shore. From the lake's inlet bridge, the trail turns left and contours the lip of the basin to a fine viewpoint for the Simpson Valley.

> **OPTION**
>
> Rather that walking up the service road to Rock Isle Lake, many hikers ride the **STANDISH CHAIRLIFT** from Sunshine Village to the Standish Viewing Deck, which sits at an elevation of 2,420 metres atop Standish Ridge.
>
> From the top of the Standish Chairlift, the trail follows the ridge for 300 metres to the Standish Viewing Deck, then descends steeply for 300 metres to the Twin Cairns-Meadow Park trail. Take the left fork and it's 400 metres to the Rock Isle-Grizzly-Larix Lakes loop junction. By starting with a ride on the Standish Chairlift and returning to Sunshine Village via the Rock Isle Lake Viewpoint, the Rock Isle-Grizzly-Larix Lakes loop is 7.2 kilometres (2 to 2.5 hours roundtrip).
>
> Energetic hikers can make a full day of it by completing the Rock Isle-Grizzly-Larix Lakes loop then hiking back to Sunshine Village via Twin Cairns-Meadow Park. This option totals around 10 kilometres.

ROCK ISLE-GRIZZLY-LARIX LAKES

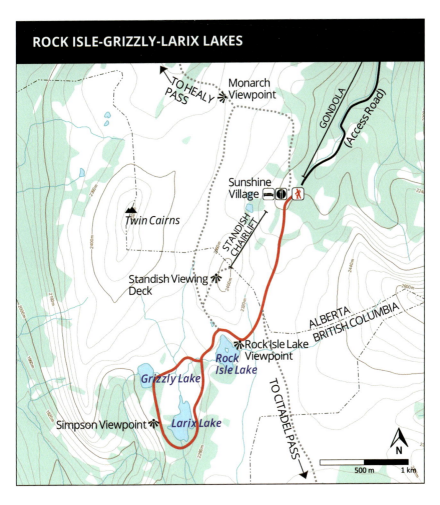

Larix, the largest of the two lakes, is just beyond the viewpoint. The lake lies between meadow and larch forest (the Latin botanical name for alpine larch is *Larix lyallii*, hence the lake's name.) You follow the shoreline before climbing back to the loop split and returning to Rock Isle Lake.

Twin Cairns-Meadow Park

Though the majority of Sunshine Village day hikers strike out on the Rock Isle-Grizzly-Larix Lakes loop, we usually combine this circuit with the less-travelled trail running beneath Twin Cairns peak to Meadow Park. Ride the Standish Chairlift to begin your adventure and you take out much of the elevation gain.

Length: 4.5 km (2.8 miles)
Elevation gain: minimal
Allow: 1.5 hours roundtrip
Rating: Easy/moderate
Map: Gem Trek
 Banff & Mount Assiniboine

Trailhead N51°04.281' W115°47.175'

For information on getting to Sunshine Village, see page 84. From Sunshine Village, continue above the Village area on the Standish Chairlift.

Trail Outline

- 0.0 Trailhead (elevation 2,420 metres).
- 0.3 Standish Viewing Deck.
  —Steep descent.
- 0.6 Junction. Rock Isle Lake left. Twin Cairns-Meadow Park right.
  —Gradual climb through alpine meadows.
- 2.8 Junction. Monarch Viewpoint left 0.1 km. Village area right.
  —Steady descent via meadows, ski run, and forest.
- 4.5 Village area (elevation 2,200 metres).

Trail Description

From Sunshine Village, ride the Standish Chairlift (included in your gondola/bus fare) to Standish Ridge. Views from the ridge are spectacular, and only improve along a 300-metre trail that leads to the Standish Viewing Deck. This lookout provides an unparalleled panorama of the Sunshine Meadows region. Rock Isle, Larix and Grizzly Lakes lie below the viewpoint to the south, while the route to Citadel Pass (page 96) can be traced across the vast meadows to the southeast to Quartz Hill and Citadel Peak. The distinctive summit of

Mount Assiniboine (3,618 metres) rises beyond Quartz Hill, and to the west a sea of peaks form the ranges of Kootenay National Park.

From the viewing deck, the trail descends 300 metres to a junction. The Twin Cairns-Meadow Park trail, which is to the right (a 600-metre each way detour to the left leads to the Rock Isle Lake Viewpoint).

From the junction below Standish Ridge, the Twin Cairns-Meadow Park trail veers off to the north and climbs through thinning forest to a shallow alpine valley between Standish Ridge and Twin Cairns. The trail runs over this flat, open meadow for nearly two kilometres to a junction with the Simpson Pass trail, passing beside small pools fringed with the white-tufts of cotton grass and crossing several small streams. Grizzly bears have visited this vale in recent years, digging up the landscape in search of tasty ground squirrels.

Views seemingly extend forever on the Twin Cairns section of the trail.

At the junction with the Simpson Pass trail, you should make the 100-metre detour to the Monarch Viewpoint (also called Wawa Summit), a shallow pass between Twin Cairns and Wawa Ridge. This is a wonderful vantage point for the impressive pyramid-peak called The Monarch to the southwest and the long ridge of Monarch Ramparts leading to Healy Pass to the west. The panorama also includes the Citadel Pass region and Mount Assiniboine to the southeast. Small ponds fringed with cotton grass dot the meadows and, like many open areas in the Sunshine region, the ridge is a wildflower-lover's dream.

As you descend back to Sunshine Village on the Meadow Park trail, there are more expansive views out across the valley to Lookout Mountain (2,730 metres), identified as Brewster Rock on topo maps; its summit forms the border between Alberta and British Columbia, and the Great Divide Express Quad that runs to a point just below the peak is Canada's highest ski lift.

Views dwindle as you make a steep descent along a ski run and then a forest trail back to Sunshine Village.

Monarch Viewpoint is well worth the short detour.

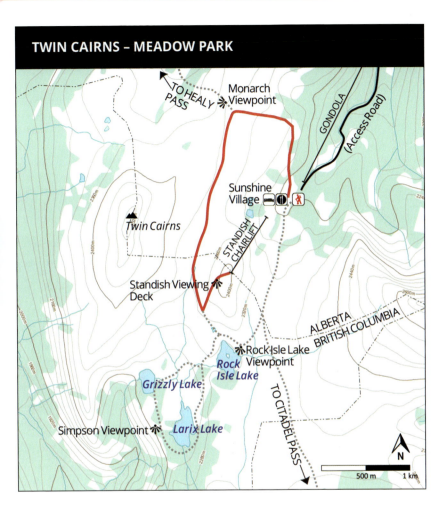

OPTION

An alternative to riding the Standish Chairlift to Standish Ridge is to walk up the service road from the Village area to **ROCK ISLE LAKE VIEWPOINT**. This is a good option if the weather is inclement. If you strike out on this option, the distance of the Twin Cairns-Meadow Park loop is 6.3 kilometres (allow two hours) and you gain 160 metres of elevation.

Looking down to Rock Isle Lake from the Standish Viewing Deck.

Citadel Pass

The trail to Citadel Pass rolls through the heart of the Sunshine Meadows, crossing and recrossing the Continental Divide, weaving back and forth between Alberta and British Columbia. Highlights include some of the finest wildflower meadows in the Canadian Rockies and an outstanding view of Mount Assiniboine.

Length: 9.3 km (5.8 miles) one way
Elevation gain: 195 metres (640 feet)
Allow: 2.5 to 3 hours one way
Rating: Moderate
Map: Gem Trek
  Banff & Mount Assiniboine

Trailhead N51°04.712′ W115°46.942′

For information on getting to Sunshine Village, see page 84. From Sunshine Village, continue above the day lodge on a gravel roadbed following the trail to Rock Isle Lake.

Trail Outline

0.0	Trailhead (elevation 2,200 metres).
	—Follow gravel road uphill.
1.2	Continental Divide (elevation 2,305 metres). Alberta-B.C. boundary.
1.3	Junction. Rock Isle Lake ahead. Citadel Pass left.
4.7	Trail begins climb to east ridge of Quartz Hill.
5.2	Quartz Hill ridge summit (elevation 2,395 metres).
5.8	Howard Douglas Lake.
7.4	Citadel Lake.
9.3	Citadel Pass (elevation 2,360 metres).

Looking down to Howard Douglas Lake from Quartz Hill.

Trail Description

The Citadel Pass trail starts from the centre of Sunshine Village and follows the same route as the Rock Isle Lake trail for the first 1.3 kilometres. Just beyond the 2,305-metre-high summit on the Continental Divide, the Citadel Pass trail branches left (Rock Isle Lake Viewpoint is only a few minutes beyond the junction and a worthwhile side trip).

From the junction you cross a vast alpine meadow for more than one kilometre before invisibly re-entering Alberta and gradually descending into scattered forest. The trail flattens out briefly across a meadow then ascends steeply through stands of alpine fir and larch to Quartz Hill's east ridge.

The lofty east ridge below the summit of Quartz Hill is a good destination for those lacking time or energy to continue farther. Howard Douglas Lake lies below the ridge to the southeast, and a long line of meadows and scattered forest stretches away beyond the lake to Citadel Pass, cradled between Citadel Peak and Fatigue Mountain.

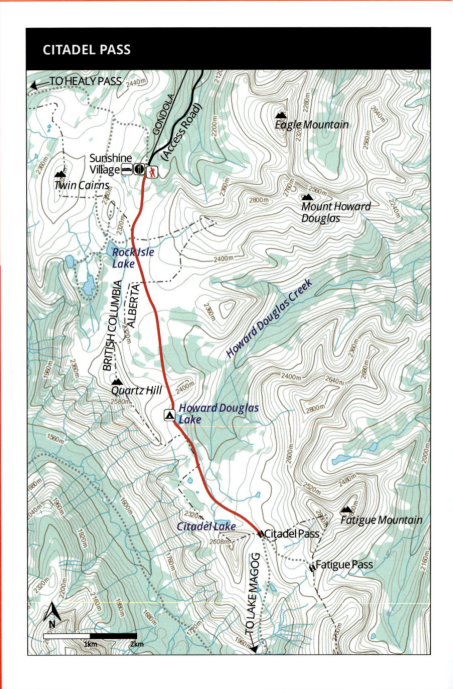

Quartz Hill was described by boundary surveyor Arthur Wheeler in 1913 as "a prominent hill, with a crest of broken blocks of quartz, falling very steeply on the south west side to form the valley of the Simpson River." It is one of several rocky promontories rising from Sunshine Meadows.

Continuing beyond the summit of Quartz Hill Ridge, the trail drops sharply to the shores of Howard Douglas Lake, a distance of 600 metres. Another small lake, Citadel, lies off to the right of the trail 1.6 kilometres beyond Howard Douglas Lake, its basin set in a gap that serves as a window to Mount Assiniboine. This is one of the best views of this famous 3,618-metre "horn" peak from the Sunshine Meadows. Though the summit seems to loom near, it is over 15 kilometres away.

You'll find yourself back on the Continental Divide and the boundary between Banff National Park (Alberta) and Mount Assiniboine Provincial Park (British Columbia) when you reach the rocky 2,360-metre summit of Citadel Pass. If only you had time to follow the 2.5-kilometre trail left to the even higher Fatigue Pass, or the 18.2-kilometre trail ahead into the heart of Mount Assiniboine Provincial Park! But even strong hikers will likely turn back on Citadel and hustle briskly to catch the last gondola car or shuttle bus down from Sunshine Village in the late afternoon.

Stopping to photograph wildflowers along the Citadel Pass trail.

Healy Pass

The hike to Healy Pass and back makes for a long day trip, but it more than compensates with vast wildflower meadows on the approach and a panorama from its summit of nearly every peak along a 70-kilometre stretch of the Continental Divide from Mount Assiniboine to Storm Mountain.

Length: 9.2 km (5.7 miles) one way
Elevation gain: 655 metres (2,150 feet)
Allow: 2.5 to 3 hours one way
Rating: Moderate/difficult
Map: Gem Trek *Banff Egypt Lake*

Trailhead N51°06.895′ W115°45.890′

Follow the Trans-Canada Highway nine km northwest from Banff, then drive nine km to the Bourgeau Base Area of Sunshine Village. The trail starts from the far parking lot behind the base station.

Trail Outline

- **0.0** Trailhead (elevation 1,675 metres).
- **0.8** Junction. Sunshine Village ahead; Healy Pass right.
- **3.1** Tributary stream bridge.
- **5.5** Healy Creek Campground.
- **5.9** Junction. Simpson Pass left 2 km; Healy Pass ahead.
—Steady climb through meadows.
- **7.7** Junction. Simpson Pass left. Healy Pass ahead.
- **9.2** Healy Pass (elevation 2,330 metres).

Trail Description

Starting from the far end of the parking lot behind the Sunshine gondola base station, the Healy Pass trail follows a wide, bulldozed track for nearly a kilometre before cutting off onto a more aesthetic forest path. Gradually, but steadily, it ascends the Healy Creek Valley, rising from a dense canopy of Engelmann spruce and alpine fir to subalpine meadows where wildflowers bloom in lush profusion from mid-July to late August. Once you enter the meadows, you make a steady climb through the last stands of alpine larch to Healy Pass.

Healy Pass is a wonderful place to enjoy flower-filled alpine meadows.

The golden glow of larch are a major draw to Healy Pass in September.

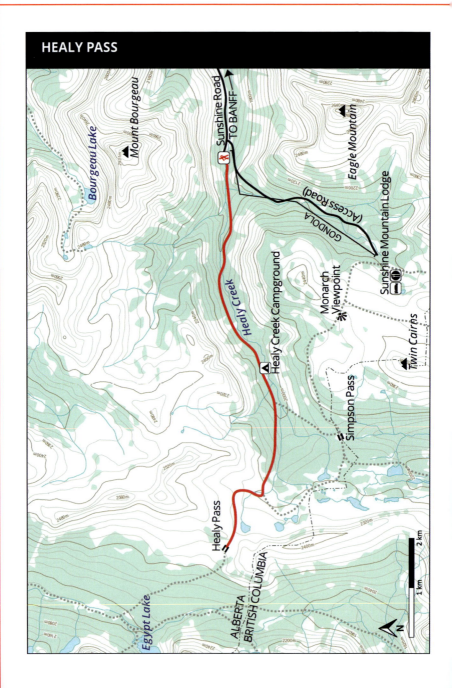

This 2,330-metre-high pass at the north end of the Monarch Ramparts ridge offers an excellent overview of the surrounding landscape. The block of peaks beyond the ridge to the northeast is the Massive Range, dominated by Mount Brett on the left and Mount Bourgeau to the right. Nearly 30 kilometres to the southeast, rising high above all its neighbouring peaks, is the "horn" of Mount Assiniboine—the highest mountain in the Canadian Rockies south of the Columbia Icefield at 3,618 metres above sea level. Less than six kilometres away, at the south end of the Monarch Ramparts, is the massive pyramid called The Monarch. Due west of the pass, stacked beneath the Pharaoh Peaks, are Egypt and Scarab Lakes.

OPTION

While Healy Pass is usually reached by ascending Healy Creek, an easier and more scenic approach is from **SUNSHINE VILLAGE** via Monarch Viewpoint. Ascending the Meadow Park trail (see page 90), the first 1.8 kilometres climbs through the upper fringes of subalpine forest to Monarch Viewpoint. Beyond the viewpoint, the trail descends back into stands of alpine fir and larch. After following beneath a low escarpment for nearly two kilometres, it drops into a small meadow on the summit of Simpson Pass. From Simpson Pass, the trail stays on the Alberta side of the divide and begins its climb to the Healy Meadows. Just before reaching the meadows, 400 metres beyond the pass, a trail branches left to Eohippus Lake—an interesting 3.2-kilometre each way side-trip for strong hikers who have time and energy to spare. Just beyond the Eohippus junction, you reach the southeastern edge of the Healy Meadows beside a small lake. The trail continues for another kilometre through lake-studded meadows beneath the long ridge of the Monarch Ramparts. You reach an intersection with the Healy Pass trail 7.8 kilometres from Sunshine Village, from where Healy Pass is 1.5 kilometres to the left.

By setting out for Healy Pass from Sunshine Village, hikers enjoy the high alpine scenery in the vicinity of Simpson Pass.

Bourgeau Lake

Set within an amphitheatre carved from the limestone walls of the Massive Range, Bourgeau Lake exhibits a variety of subalpine and alpine scenery, flowers and wildlife. Ptarmigan, marmots and pikas pursue their daily chores in the rockslides bordering the lake, and in early summer, avalanches thunder down over Mount Bourgeau's cliffs above. A spectacular setting, indeed!

Length: 7.5 km (4.6 miles) one way
Elevation gain: 725 metres (2,380 feet)
Allow: 2.5 to 3 hours one way
Rating: Moderate/difficult
Map: Gem Trek *Banff Egypt Lake*

Trailhead N51°10.086′ W115°43.895′

Follow the Trans-Canada Highway northwest from the town of Banff for 11 km (2.8 km northwest of the Sunshine Village interchange). A cross-over road provides access from westbound lanes to the trailhead.

Trail Outline

- **0.0** Trailhead (elevation 1,435 metres).
  —Begin steady switchbacking climb.
- **1.6** Switchbacks end.
- **3.7** Tributary stream bridge.
- **5.5** Wolverine Creek crossing. Cascades. Begin steep switchbacks.
- **6.8** Trail levels out into meadows.
- **7.5** Bourgeau Lake (elevation 2,160 metres).

Trail Description

Striking off from a parking area beside the Trans-Canada Highway, the trail quickly buries itself in a forest of lodgepole pine and spruce, and after quickly gaining elevation via a series of switchbacks, climbs steadily along the southeast side of the Wolverine Creek Valley. Views soon open back to the Bow Valley and the sharp, serrated peaks of the Sawback Range. The broad summit of Mount Brett (2,984 metres), the highest mountain in the Massive Range, dominates the scene ahead.

Around 5.5 kilometres from the trailhead, the trail crosses Wolverine Creek, where the stream descends from the Bourgeau Lake cirque in a series of cascades. The foot of the waterfall is a good spot for rest and refreshment before tackling the steep switchbacks that complete the climb to a long, stream-side meadow leading to the lake.

The amphitheatre containing the lake is carved into the northwest side of Mount Bourgeau (2,930 metres). Like other peaks in the range, its cliffs are formed by Devonian and Mississippian limestones and shales—formations bearing fossils of brachiopods, corals, and other examples of early ocean

Wolverine Creek crossing.

Bourgeau Lake.

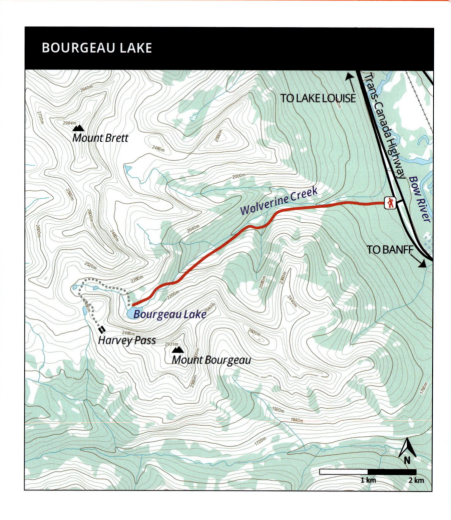

life. Dr. James Hector named the mountain for the French botanist Eugene Bourgeau, his comrade-in-exploration with the Palliser Expedition during the summer of 1858.

Snowbanks often linger in the meadows bordering the lake until mid-July, their meltwaters feeding a wide variety of subalpine wildflowers. White-tailed ptarmigan are sometimes seen along the lake's outlet stream or in the nearby talus slopes, their mottled summer plumage making them all but invisible among the piles of broken rock. Pikas, golden-mantled ground squirrels and chipmunks scurry back and forth through the boulders, closely watching passing hikers for a possible handout.

OPTION

You can explore above the lake to **HARVEY PASS**, which lies 2.2 kilometres beyond Bourgeau Lake and 294-vertical metres higher up. A path follows above the forested north shore of Bourgeau Lake then climbs steeply toward the obvious notch where a stream drops from between Mounts Bourgeau and Brett. After some strenuous climbing, the track skirts a small, rockbound lake and emerges into an open alpine bowl complete with small ponds.

While this lofty cirque is quite pleasant, you will want to continue climbing south to the obvious pass at the foot of Mount Bourgeau's long summit ridge. In less than 15 minutes you crest Harvey Pass (2,454 metres) and are greeted with an exceptional view south to the towering pyramid of Mount Assiniboine. Harvey Lake is a small tarn cradled on the summit and, like the pass, is named for Ralph Harvey, who was a manager for Banff's Brewster Transport Co. and involved in the development of skiing at nearby Sunshine Village.

The view at Harvey Pass.

Shadow Lake

Situated beneath the massive cliffs of Mount Ball, Shadow Lake is one of the largest and most impressive lakes along the Continental Divide. A few people complete the long hike to the lake and back in a day, or they bike-and-hike, since mountain bikes are permitted as far as Pharaoh Creek junction.

Length: 14 km (8.7 miles) one way
Elevation gain: 452 metres (1,480 feet)
Allow: 3.5 to 4.5 hours one way
Rating: Moderate/difficult
Map: Gem Trek *Banff Egypt Lake*

Trailhead N51°13.206′ W115°48.227′

Redearth Creek trailhead parking area, along the Trans-Canada Highway 20 km northwest of the town of Banff and 10.5 km southeast of Castle Junction.

Trail Outline

0.0	Trailhead (elevation 1,400 metres).
0.4	Trail joins old roadbed.
6.9	Redearth Creek bridge. Lost Horse Creek Campground.
10.5	Junction (bike rack). Pharaoh Creek trail left. Shadow Lake right.
12.7	Shadow Lake Campground.
12.8	Shadow Lake Lodge.
13.0	Junction. Gibbon Pass right. Shadow Lake ahead.
14.0	Shadow Lake (elevation 1,852 metres).

Trail Description

The first three-quarters of the trip follow the broad track of the old talc-mining road constructed up Redearth and Pharaoh Creeks in the late 1920s. The hiking is somewhat tedious, but the climb is gradual and it is easy to make good time.

At 10.5 kilometres, the Shadow Lake trail branches right from the roadbed and climbs into the forest. (Bikes are not permitted beyond this junction, and a rack is provided for lock-up.) From the junction it is 2.3 kilometres to Shadow Lake Lodge. The trail continues up-valley beyond the lodge and soon reaches a bridge over the lake's outlet stream.

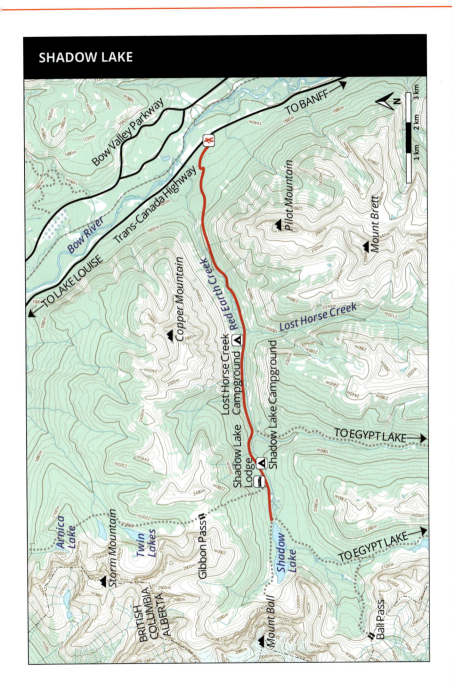

Shadow Lake.

Shadow Lake Lodge.

Shadow Lake is large compared with most subalpine lakes, stretching for over two kilometres to the base of Mount Ball (3,311 metres). Carved from Cambrian limestone and quartzite formations and draped with glaciers, the mountain provides a photogenic backdrop.

Most of the trails beyond Shadow Lake, such as the wildflower meadows of **GIBBON PASS** and the solitude of **BALL PASS**, can only be considered by those who overnight at Shadow Lake Lodge (shadowlakelodge.com), a delightful backcountry accommodation set in an open meadow just over one kilometre from the lake.

Arnica Lake

Though the distance for this hike is not great, it is arduous—dropping to the shores of Vista Lake and then climbing steadily to Arnica Lake. Yet, despite all its ups-and-downs, the hike to this tarn nestled beneath the east face of Storm Mountain is popular and well worth the effort.

Length: 5 km (3.1 miles) one way
Elevation gain: 580 metres (1,900 feet)
Allow: 1.5 to 2 hours one way
Rating: Moderate
Map: Gem Trek *Banff Egypt Lake*

Trailhead N51°14.476′ W116°02.131′

The trailhead is a small parking lot along Highway 93 South 8 km west of Castle Junction and 2 km east of Vermilion Pass.

Trail Outline

0.0	Trailhead (elevation 1,690 metres).
	—Steady downhill.
1.4	Vista Lake outlet (elevation 1,570 metres).
	—Moderate to steep uphill begins.
4.2	Small pond.
5.0	Arnica Lake (elevation 2,150 metres).

Trail Description

Starting from Highway 93 South, the Arnica Lake trail descends steadily through dense, fire-succession lodgepole pine forest. It soon reaches its lowest elevation beside Vista Lake, a peaceful green body of water that is a pleasant destination for less energetic hikers. You will want to spend some time here relaxing and enjoying the scene before tackling the steep climb ahead.

From the lake's outlet bridge, the trail climbs eastward across the lower slopes of Storm Mountain. Views along this stretch were quite open for a couple of decades after the 1968 Vermilion Pass burn, but like the descent to Vista Lake, pine forest is enclosing the trail once more. Around four kilometres from the trailhead, you enter a mature subalpine forest, and not long after passing a small pond you reach the shores of Arnica Lake.

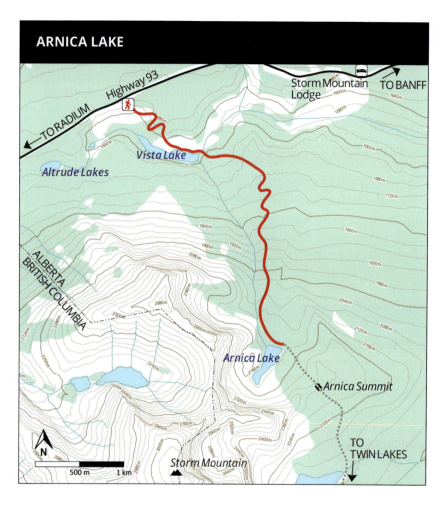

Arnica Lake is backed against the sheer cliffs of Storm Mountain and enclosed on three sides by a typical upper subalpine forest of Engelmann spruce and alpine fir with a scattering of larch. Its name comes from the yellow-flowered arnica, which blooms in this cool, moist forest during early summer.

Arnica Lake is backed by the steep cliffs of Storm Mountain.

OPTION

From the lake's outlet the trail climbs for 800 metres to **ARNICA SUMMIT**, a forested ridge extending northeastward from Storm Mountain. By leaving the trail and climbing along the ridge to the southwest, you are rewarded with extensive views north and south along the Bow Valley.

This trail continues over Arnica Summit to **TWIN LAKES**, reaching Upper Twin Lake after a steady 1.4-kilometre descent from the summit, and Lower Twin Lake lies just 800 metres beyond. The Twin Lakes are just as striking as Arnica, with a similar backdrop created by Storm Mountain cliffs and lush wildflower meadows along their eastern shores. But remember, you will have a strenuous up-down-up hike on the way back. If you have two vehicles, an option is to use the Twin Lakes trail as an alternative route back to Highway 93. The total distance between Vista Lake viewpoint and the Twin Lakes trailhead is 16 kilometres.

Upper Twin Lake.

Boom Lake

The Boom Lake trail is an easy walk to a beautifully formed lake contained by a massive 600-metre-high limestone wall and glacier-mantled peaks. The trail is often snow-free in early June, which makes it a popular early season outing. But it is often muddy, so good footwear is recommended.

Length: 5.1 km (3.2 miles) one way
Elevation gain: 175 metres (575 feet)
Allow: 1.5 hours one way
Rating: Easy
Map: Gem Trek
  Banff & Mount Assiniboine

Trailhead N51°14.951′ W116°01.455′

Follow Highway 93 South 7 km west from Castle Junction to the signposted Boom Lake trailhead parking area. The trail begins from the bridge at the rear of the parking lot.

Trail Outline

- **0.0** Trailhead (elevation 1,720 metres).
  —Trail crosses Boom Creek bridge and begins steady, moderate climb through forest on broad track.
- **5.0** Trail narrows.
- **5.1** Boom Lake (elevation 1,895 metres).

Trail Description

For most of its length the trail is a wide, bulldozed track that climbs at a moderate grade well above the creek. In the spring many small streams make the trail a bit sloppy, but the runoff redeems itself by creating a well-watered forest with lush undergrowth and wildflowers.

Just before the trail reaches the lake it narrows to a traditional footpath, and a short distance beyond it ends abruptly at a rockslide that has tumbled down from the slope to the north into the eastern end of the lake. A bit of rock-hopping will get you to the water's edge.

The broad north face of Boom Mountain soars above the lake's south shore, and the glaciated spires of Quadra Mountain (3,173 metres) and Bident Mountain

BOOM LAKE

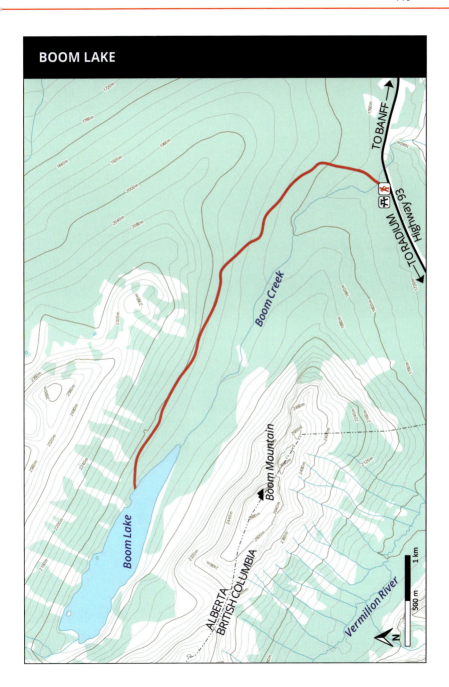

Boom Lake.

(3,084 metres) rise beyond its far end. If you visit the lake in late spring or early summer, you will likely see avalanches cascading down Boom Mountain's north face.

The Alpine Club of Canada held its annual camp at nearby Vermilion Pass in 1912, and later documented how Boom Lake received its name: "Boom Lake is so called from the fact that near its eastern extremity an old moraine, at one time the bounding wall of the lake, now just touches the surface which has overflowed it. It spans the lake in a crescent, some distance from the eastern end, and intercepts the driftwood floating down the lake. The appearance created is that of a lumber boom, and hence the name."

Look to the east when you arrive at trail's end and you'll see the log boom for which the lake is named.

Taylor Lake

Taylor Lake is one of the most accessible of several hanging-valley lakes along the southwest side of the Bow Valley between Banff and Lake Louise. It is every bit as scenic as nearby lakes and offers the added bonus of two attractive side-trips from its shores.

Length: 6.6 km (4.1 miles) one way
Elevation gain: 585 metres (1,925 feet)
Allow: 2 hours one way
Rating: Moderate
Map: Gem Trek
Banff & Mount Assiniboine

Trailhead N51°18.310′ W116°01.270′

The trailhead for Taylor Lake is signposted along the Trans-Canada Highway 8 km northwest of Castle Junction and 17.5 km southeast of Lake Louise.

Trail Outline

- **0.0** Trailhead (elevation 1,480 metres).
- **1.3** Taylor Creek bridge.
  —Steady uphill begins.
- **6.1** Taylor Creek bridge.
- **6.4** Junction. O'Brien Lake left. Taylor Lake ahead.
- **6.5** Taylor Lake (elevation 2,065 metres).

Trail Description

The Taylor Lake hike begins from a parking area 400 metres east of Taylor Creek and follows near the highway's wildlife-control fence before bending west and coming abreast of the creek. The rest of the trip to the lake is straightforward and not particularly inspiring, travelling over a broad track that switchbacks steadily up the side of the valley through a closed forest of lodgepole pine and spruce. As the trail nears the lake, it is often quite muddy.

Taylor Lake is well worth the drudgery of the climb as the trail suddenly emerges into meadow near the lake's outlet—a moist area carpeted with western anemone, marsh marigold, buttercups, and mountain laurel through much of the summer. Fringing the meadow and much of the lakeshore is a typical

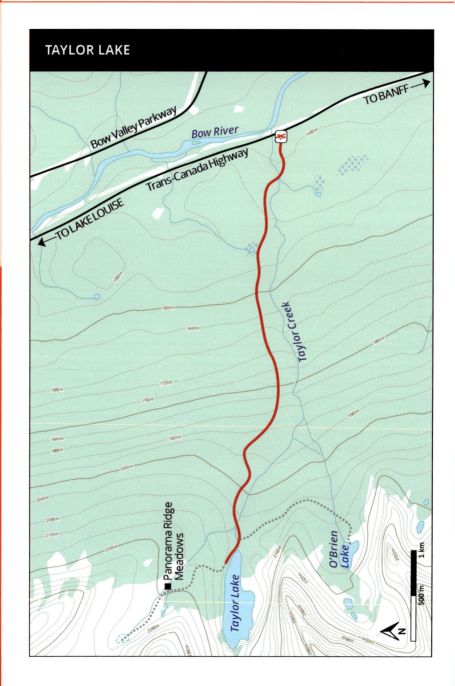

upper-subalpine forest of alpine fir and Engelmann spruce dotted with the pale green, summer foliage of alpine larch (golden in September).

Taylor Lake.

The north face of Mount Bell rises abruptly from the south shore of the lake, forming a 750-metre-high wall. The low notch of Taylor Pass to the west separates Mount Bell from Panorama Ridge and serves as a rock scrambler's route to Consolation Valley and Moraine Lake.

OPTION

For strong hikers, there are two options beyond Taylor Lake worth considering.

O'BRIEN LAKE is in a smaller cirque 2.1 kilometres to the south of Taylor Lake. With a more lavish display of wildflowers along its shore and more alpine larch in the surrounding forest, it can be even more charming than Taylor. To reach the lake cross Taylor Creek at the trail sign just below Taylor Lake. Follow the rocky but well-travelled track that drops below Mount Bell's cliffs and then climbs steeply to the level of the O'Brien cirque. Watch for a sign indicating the junction where the O'Brien trail branches to the right. The short side-trail all but disappears in the boggy meadows, but by staying along the left side of the lake's outlet stream you soon reach your destination.

By following the trail leading north from Taylor Lake Campground for 15 minutes or so (a steep, steady climb), you can visit **PANORAMA RIDGE MEADOWS**, one of the great wildflower meadows and larch forests in the Canadian Rockies. The snow-streaked cliffs of Panorama Ridge serve as a backdrop to this long, gently rising meadow, which in summer is quite verdant and filled with the tall showy blooms associated with snowbed plant communities. In mid-September, the surrounding forest is awash with gold as the larch trees reach their autumn colour peak.

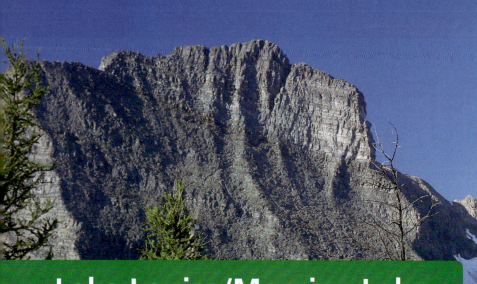

Lake Louise/Moraine Lake

Simply put, there are few hiking areas in the world that can rival the Lake Louise/Moraine Lake region. These two lakes, stunning destinations themselves, provide the starting point for a great variety of trails leading through some of the most rugged yet accessible alpine scenery imaginable. The most popular destination from Lake Louise is Lake Agnes, while Larch Valley is the target for many Moraine Lake hikers. Two backcountry tea houses make these trails even more appealing.

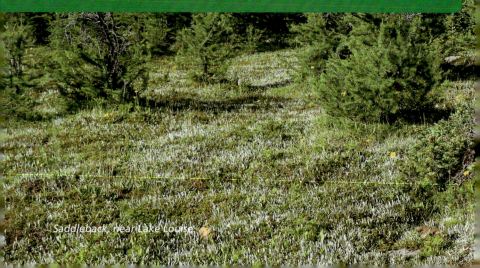

Saddleback, near Lake Louise.

Lake Agnes

Delightful Lake Agnes is hidden in a hanging valley high above Lake Louise. In addition to its own charms, which include a tea house, the lake and the nearby Beehives provide breathtaking views of Lake Louise and a broad stretch of the Bow Valley.

Length: 3.5 km (2.2 miles) one way
Elevation gain: 405 metres (1,325 feet)
Allow: 1 hour one way
Rating: Easy/moderate
Map: Gem Trek *Best of Lake Louise*

Trailhead N51°25.044' W116°13.160'

Follow the paved shoreline trail in front of Chateau Lake Louise north 200 metres to the Lake Agnes trail, leading uphill to the right.

Trail Outline

0.0	Trailhead (elevation 1,730 metres).
	—Steady uphill on broad track.
1.7	Switchback. View to Lake Louise.
2.5	Junction. Horse trail intersects from right.
2.6	Mirror Lake. Junction. Highline trail left. Lake Agnes right. Switchbacks begin.
3.2	Junction. Little Beehive shortcut right. Lake Agnes ahead.
3.5	Lake Agnes and Tea House (elevation 2,135 metres).

Trail Description

For the first half hour from the shore of Lake Louise, the Lake Agnes trail follows a broad, moderately graded trail through dense subalpine forest. At 1.7 kilometres the first switchback marks a break in the trees where you have a clear view down to the pale turquoise waters of Lake Louise.

Another 800 metres brings you to Mirror Lake—a tiny sink lake that takes its name from its round looking-glass appearance. The dark, layered cliffs of Big Beehive loom above, and, in the gap to the right, the roof of Lake Agnes Tea House is barely visible.

By taking the Plain of the Six Glaciers highline trail to the left at the Mirror Lake junction, you can make a direct ascent to Lake Agnes via a steep trail that traverses the rockslide beneath Big Beehive. (This short cut branches right from the highline trail 150 metres beyond this junction.) But if this steep trail is wet, icy or snowy, avoid it and follow the traditional route that branches right at Mirror Lake (it's only 200 metres longer).

Regardless of which option you choose, the journey to Lake Agnes is completed on one of two steep, wooden staircases that surmount a cliff band beside the waterfall created by the lake's outlet stream.

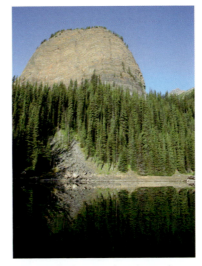

Mirror Lake is a good resting point before making the final push to Lake Agnes.

Lake Agnes in fall.

Lake Agnes.

Lake Agnes Tea House.

Arriving at the narrow opening where Lake Agnes tumbles from its basin, the entire length of the lake suddenly appears, stretching westward to a jagged backdrop created by Mounts Whyte (2,983 metres) and Niblock (2,976 metres). The tea house sits atop the cliff on the north side of the outlet stream, just a few metres from the lake.

The original **LAKE AGNES TEA HOUSE** was constructed shortly after the turn of the 20th century. The present-day version was built in 1981. It serves refreshments and light snacks from mid-June to early October and is one of the attractions for many who do this hike. While its covered porch is a relaxing place to sit and admire the view, it is usually a very busy place. (We like to stop there shortly after it opens at 8 am or just before 5 pm closing to avoid the crowds.)

Many hikers end their day with a stroll along the shore of Lake Agnes to its boulder-strewn western end, only 800 metres beyond the tea house.

NOTE: The parking lot at Lake Louise is often full by 8am in summer. Page 20 has information on alternative methods for getting to Lake Louise.

OPTIONS

The most popular short hike beyond Lake Agnes is to the **LITTLE BEEHIVE**. Though not as high as the nearby Big Beehive, it provides better views of both Lake Louise and the Bow Valley, and you won't work as hard to get there. The 900-metre trail branches uphill from the Lake Agnes shoreline trail just beyond the tea house. It climbs steadily to the northeast through alpine fir and larch and across avalanche slopes. Stands of larch become thicker as you climb, making this a very rewarding trip in the last two weeks of September when their needles turn to gold.

Another option is the 1.6-kilometre trail from the tea house to the **BIG BEEHIVE**. The Lake Agnes trail continues around the far end of the lake and climbs a steep series of switchbacks to a junction on the Big Beehive summit ridge. Traverse eastward along the rocky, lightly forested ridge to a gazebo-style shelter on the northeast edge of the 2,255-metre-high promontory. Though somewhat obscured by trees, there are views over the Bow Valley and down to Lake Louise, over 500 metres below. (Do not attempt to shortcut down from the gazebo viewpoint in any direction; there are dangerous cliffs on all sides. Return back along the ridge the way you came.)

The **LAKE AGNES-PLAIN OF THE SIX GLACIERS CIRCUIT** is a 14.5-kilometre hike that combines the two most popular trails from Lake Louise. Cross the Big Beehive's summit ridge at the viewpoint trail junction and follow a steep trail down the south side. Reaching the highline trail running up-valley from Mirror Lake, turn right and follow it as it descends across the lower slopes of Devil's Thumb to an intersection with the Plain of the Six Glaciers trail. Continue up-valley another 1.4 kilometres to the Plain of the Six Glaciers Tea House (see page 128).

Big Beehive.

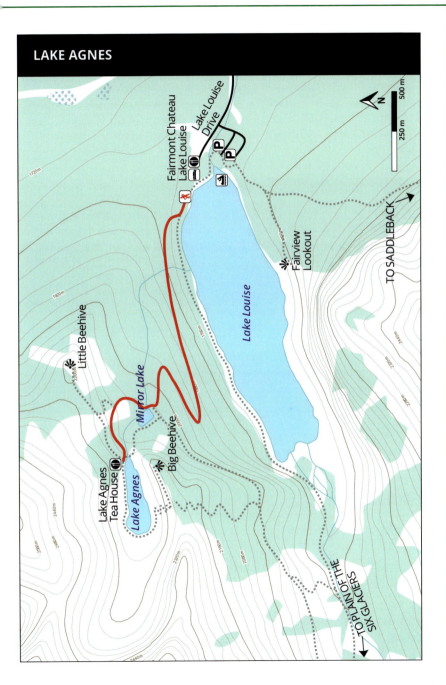

Plain of the Six Glaciers

The Plain of the Six Glaciers trail leads into the Canadian Rockies' most famous postcard view beneath the glacier-capped summits of Mounts Victoria and Lefroy, where you can stop for refreshments at one of the Rockies' oldest backcountry tea houses. However, don't expect solitude on this very popular trail.

Length: 5.5 km (3.4 miles) one way
Elevation gain: 360 metres (1,180 feet)
Allow: 1.5 to 2 hours one way
Rating: Moderate
Map: Gem Trek *Best of Lake Louise*

Trailhead N51°25.044' W116°13.160'

Follow the paved shoreline trail in front of Chateau Lake Louise north to the trail sign for the Lake Louise Lakeshore, Plain of the Six Glaciers and Lake Agnes trails.

Trail Outline

- **0.0** Trailhead (elevation 1,730 metres).
  —Follow Lake Louise Lakeshore trail.
- **1.9** West end of Lake Louise.
- **2.4** Steady climb begins.
- **3.3** Junction. Big Beehive shortcut right. Plain of the Six Glaciers ahead.
- **4.1** Junction. Highline trail and Big Beehive right. Plain of the Six Glaciers ahead.
- **5.5** Plain of the Six Glaciers Tea House (elevation 2,090 metres).

Trail Description

The first section of the Plain of the Six Glaciers trail follows the busy lakeshore trail to the far end of Lake Louise. Beyond the lake's silty inlet, the crowds thin as the trail climbs steadily through subalpine forest and across the occasional avalanche path. Eventually it emerges into a landscape scoured by the Victoria Glacier, where views open to Mounts Victoria and Lefroy.

After passing the intersection with the Highline trail from Mirror Lake and the Big Beehive, you ascend along the edge of old glacial moraines. A final

Looking back to Lake Louise from the Plain of the Six Glaciers trail.

series of steep switchbacks lead up through a band of alpine fir and larch to the tea house.

The Plain of the Six Glaciers Tea House was constructed by the CPR in the mid-1920s. Refreshments and light snacks are served throughout the summer season, and its verandah is an ideal vantage point for the frequent avalanches thundering off Mounts Lefroy and Victoria in the early summer. If the tea house is overflowing with visitors, as it often is, you can relax in the clearing below the tea house and scan the nearby boulder-field for hoary marmots and pikas.

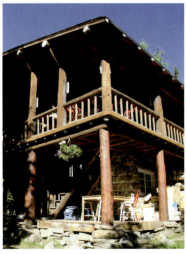
Plain of the Six Glaciers Tea House.

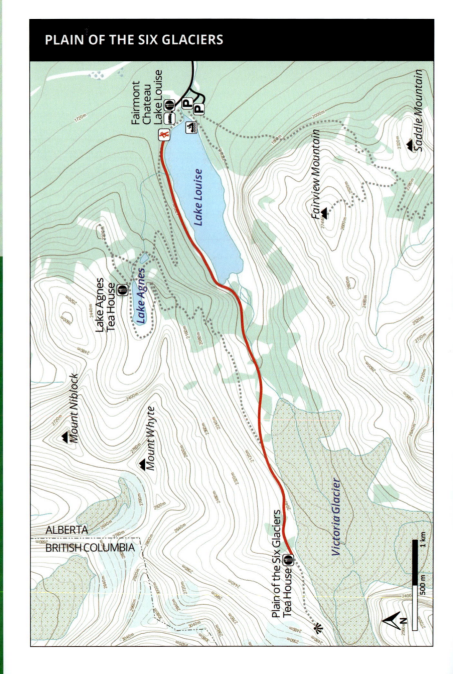

NOTE: The parking lot at Lake Louise is often full by 8am in summer. Page 20 has information on alternative methods for getting to Lake Louise.

OPTION

The Plain of the Six Glaciers trail continues up-valley beyond the tea house for another 1.3 kilometres to the **ABBOT PASS VIEWPOINT** (allow 20 minutes each way). Along the way it traverses the crest of a lateral moraine—a steep ridge of debris formed during the last advance of the Victoria Glacier, which reached its zenith during the mid-1800s. Today it provides an excellent viewpoint for the rock and boulder-covered ice of the Victoria Glacier below.

Beyond the moraine, the trail fizzles out on a steep talus slope. While this slope is a rather precarious resting spot, it is the best viewpoint for Abbot Pass (2,922 metres) between the towering summits of Mount Victoria and Mount Lefroy and the Abbot Pass Hut—a substantial stone structure constructed by CPR Swiss guides in 1922 as an overnight shelter for mountaineers. Today it is operated by the Alpine Club of Canada and is Canada's highest National Historic Site.

Heading up to the Abbot Pass Viewpoint.

The steep, ice-filled couloir rising from the Victoria Glacier to the pass is known as "The Death Trap", so-named by early mountaineers because avalanches frequently fall into it from the cliffs above. (Don't even dream of heading in that direction unless you are an experienced, well-equipped mountaineer and have checked with Parks Canada about current route conditions.)

Saddleback

The hike to Saddleback is the steepest and most demanding hike from the shores of Lake Louise. It is also one of the most rewarding, boasting the best viewpoint for Mount Temple's massive north face, wildflower meadows, and stands of golden-needled alpine larch in late September.

Length: 3.7 km (2.3 miles) one way
Elevation gain: 600 metres (1,965 feet)
Allow: 1.5 to 2 hours one way
Rating: Moderate/difficult
Map: Gem Trek *Best of Lake Louise*

Trailhead N51°24.969' W116°12.964'

From the exhibit area between Lake Louise's outlet bridge and the boathouse, the trail veers off to the left. Park in the Upper Lake Louise Lot and the trail passes right by.

Trail Outline

- **0.0** Trailhead (elevation 1,730 metres).
- **0.3** Junction. Fairview Lookout right. Saddleback ahead.
- **0.4** Junction. Moraine Lake-Paradise Valley left. Saddleback ahead.
- **1.1** Avalanche path.
  —Moderate to steep uphill begins.
- **2.7** Alpine larch stands.
- **3.7** Saddleback summit (elevation 2,330 metres).

Trail Description

In its early stages the Saddleback trail climbs steadily through the forest. At the end of the first kilometre it crosses a major avalanche path on Fairview Mountain's northeast slopes, where you have a view back to the Chateau Lake Louise and distant Mount Hector. Farther along, the trail angles up to the southwest and begins the final steep, switchbacking ascent to the pass.

Views improve just below the summit, stretching down the length of the Bow Valley to the mountains near the town of Banff. You also pass through a stand of unusually large and very old, alpine larch (core samples from similar trees in nearby Larch Valley reveal ages of more than 400 years).

Saddleback is a pleasant upland meadow where buttercups, western anemone, alpine speedwell and many other wildflowers bloom in early summer. The towering north wall of Mount Temple (3,544 metres), the third highest mountain in Banff National Park, dominates the view south of the pass.

The best view of Mount Temple, looming over tiny Lake Annette and Paradise Valley, is found a short distance southeast of the trail along the summit ridge. Follow a

The final approach is through open stands of larch, allowing expansive views.

Golden larch brighten the landscape of Saddleback each September.

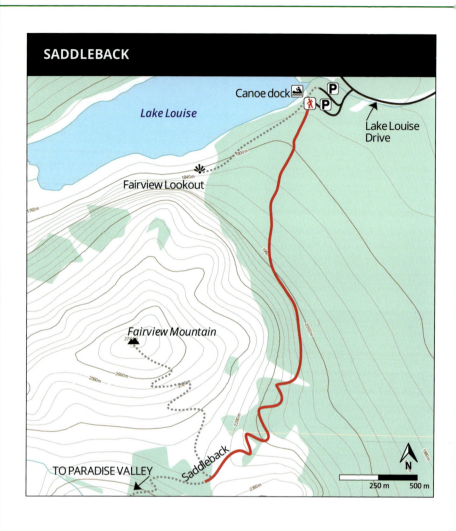

faint path through scrub alpine fir to a viewpoint with a pair of large boulders overlooking Sheol Valley—a classic alpine viewpoint that has even been exploited by Hollywood (John Barrymore gripped his leading lady Camilla Horn in a passionate embrace here during the filming of *Eternal Love* in August, 1928).

NOTE: The parking lot at Lake Louise is often full by 8am in summer. Page 20 has information on alternative methods for getting to Lake Louise.

Mount Temple and the sheer east face of Sheol Mountain dominate the view on the Saddleback.

OPTION

With the glacier-crowned summits of Mount Victoria, Mount Temple and Sheol Mountain close by, and the turquoise waters of Lake Louise a vertical kilometre below, the 2,745-metre summit of **FAIRVIEW MOUNTAIN** offers a true alpine experience. The peak is arguably the highest trail-accessible point in the mountain parks, though the 1.3-kilometre track scratched up its rocky slope many decades ago has largely disappeared. Follow faint trail northwest from Saddleback summit to begin the ascent. Continue upwards on often vague, switchbacking track, or simply scramble over loose rock towards the obvious summit. (You may have to skirt snowbanks early in the season.)

Paradise Valley

A 10.3-kilometre trail runs up Paradise Valley from the Moraine Lake Road to the Giant Steps cascades. While it's possible to hike to the Giant Steps and back in a long day, most opt for a more modest and scenic objective, Lake Annette beneath the imposing north wall of Mount Temple.

Length: 10.3 km (6.4 miles) one way
Elevation gain: 385 metres (1,250 feet)
Allow: 3 hours one way
Rating: Moderate
Map: Gem Trek *Lake Louise & Yoho*

Trailhead N51°23.763' W116°10.306'

Follow Lake Louise Drive from the village of Lake Louise three km to the junction with the Moraine Lake Road. Follow Moraine Lake Road 2.5 km to the Paradise Valley parking area.

Trail Outline

- **0.0** Trailhead (elevation 1,720 metres).
- **1.1** Junction. Moraine Lake left. Paradise Valley right.
- **1.3** Junction. Lake Louise ahead (4.0 km). Paradise Valley left.
- **3.4** Paradise Creek bridge.
- **3.9** Paradise Creek bridge.
- **4.2** Junction. Saddleback via Sheol Valley right 4.1 km.
- **5.1** Paradise Creek bridge.
- **5.7** Lake Annette (elevation 1,965 metres).
- **6.5** Trail summit (elevation 2,105 metres).
- **8.4** Junction. Sentinel Pass ahead 2.7 km. Giant Steps right.
- **9.1** Paradise Creek bridge, junction. Horseshoe Meadows left. Giant Steps ahead.
- **9.5** Junction. Horseshoe Meadows left. Giant Steps ahead.
- **10.1** Junction. Paradise Valley Campground left (0.2 km). Giant Steps ahead.
- **10.3** Giant Steps (elevation 2,000 metres).

Trail Description

When Walter Wilcox and his companions climbed to the summit of Mitre Col from Lake Louise in 1894, they looked into "a valley of surpassing beauty, wide

The first of three Paradise Creek crossings on the approach to Lake Annette.

and beautiful, with alternating open meadows and rich forests." They named it Paradise.

The first three kilometres of trail are forest-enclosed, but at the first Paradise Creek bridge, views open to Mount Temple. In another kilometre, you cross back to the northwest side of the creek and pass the Sheol Valley-Saddleback junction. At km 5.1, the trail crosses the creek once more followed by a short but strenuous ascent to Lake Annette.

Lake Annette's rocky surroundings are typical of many subalpine tarns, but its backdrop is extraordinary—the ice-capped, 1,200-metre-high north face of Mount Temple. This wall is one of the most difficult ascents in North America and remained unclimbed until 1966. And if you see one of the massive avalanches that sweep the face, you will understand one reason why.

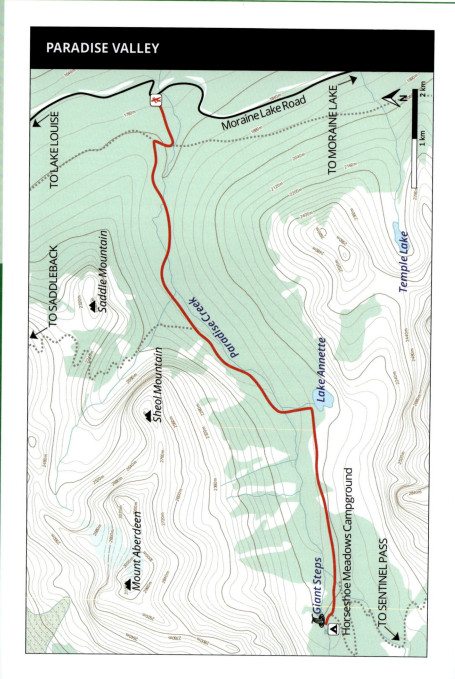

The trail continues west from Lake Annette, climbing through stands of alpine larch at the base of Mount Temple. Even if you don't plan on hiking to the Giant Steps, it's worthwhile continuing another 15 minutes or so beyond the lake to the trail's summit atop a major rockslide. Here views open to the valley headwall—Hungabee Mountain, Ringrose Peak, and Horseshoe Glacier—scenery that is blithely ignored by the marmots and pikas inhabiting the surrounding boulder field.

Nearly two kilometres beyond the trail summit, you reach a cutoff trail to the Giant Steps. This trail descends to a bridge over Paradise Creek then angles directly across the valley to the Giant Steps and Paradise Valley Campground. Sections of old trail loop further up-valley to the head of the Horseshoe Meadows, but there seems little reason to hike this slightly longer route.

Nearing the Giant Steps, you pass the branch trail to Paradise Valley Campground. Stay right and, just 200 metres beyond this junction, reach the Giant Steps—a remarkable staircase waterfall on the north fork of Paradise Creek. The falls have been photographed many times over the years, but some of the earliest images were made by members of the Alpine Club of Canada, who held their second annual camp here in 1907.

NOTES: Travel in Paradise Valley may require a group of four people hiking in close proximity to one another if special restrictions concerning grizzly bears are in place. Ask at the Lake Louise Visitor Centre if this restriction is in place, or check the trailhead kiosk for more information.

When Moraine Lake Road is closed due to a full parking lot at Moraine Lake, the closure applies to all traffic on the road and therefore it is not possible to reach the Paradise Valley trailhead. Plan on arriving before 7am to access to the Paradise Valley trailhead.

OPTION

At the 8.4-kilometre junction, take the left branch that continues along the southeast side of the valley. In another 400 metres, you reach **SENTINEL PASS** junction. The pass lies a very steep and rocky 2.3 kilometres up to the left. Most hikers find it less strenuous to climb to Sentinel Pass from Moraine Lake and then descend to Paradise Valley. This 17-kilometre traverse between Moraine Lake and the Paradise Valley trailhead is fairly popular with parties who can arrange transportation. (See Larch Valley trail, page 142.)

Giant Steps.

Larch Valley

This meadowland above Moraine Lake, with its dense stands of alpine larch and panoramic overview of the Ten Peaks, is exquisite. And above the valley, amid stark pinnacles of rock, is 2,611-metre Sentinel Pass—the highest point reached by a major trail in the Canadian Rockies.

Length: 4.5 km (2.8 miles) one way
Elevation gain: 550 metres (1,800 feet)
Allow: 1.5 to 2 hours one way
Rating: Moderate
Map: Gem Trek *Lake Louise & Yoho*

Trailhead N51°19.673' W116°10.899'

Follow Moraine Lake Road 12.5 km to the parking area at Moraine Lake. Walk to the lakeshore and the trail sign below the lodge.

Trail Outline

- **0.0** Trailhead (elevation 1,887 metres).
  —Follow Moraine Lakeshore trail.
- **0.2** Junction. Larch Valley right.
- **1.1** Switchbacks begin. Steady climb.
- **2.4** Junction. Eiffel Lake trail left. Larch Valley right.
  —Climb into Larch Valley meadows.
- **4.5** Upper Minnestimma Lake (elevation 2,435 metres).

Trail Description

From Moraine Lake the trail climbs through a forest of Engelmann spruce and alpine fir, following a steadily ascending series of switchbacks much of the way. At kilometre 2.4 the trail branches right from the Eiffel Lake trail and immediately enters the lower meadows of Larch Valley.

This high valley is the main focus for most hikers who walk the trail, and in late September, when alpine larch needles have turned to gold, it is one of the most visited trails in the Canadian Rockies. In mid-summer, however, the larch needles are a pale green and the meadows are carpeted with wildflowers.

Larch Valley in fall.

Most hikers will want to explore the entire vale to **UPPER MINNESTIMMA LAKE**, which lies above the last trees at the foot of Sentinel Pass. Looking south from this high meadowland, the heavily-glaciated Wenkchemna Peaks (Valley of the Ten Peaks) stretch across the horizon, providing one of the most striking panoramas in the Canadian Rockies.

NOTES: Travel on the Larch Valley trail may require a group of four people hiking in close proximity to one another if special restrictions concerning grizzly bears are in place. These will be posted at the Lake Louise Visitor Centre and at the trailhead.

Moraine Lake Road is closed when the Moraine Lake parking area is full. This often happens as early as 7am, so plan on arriving early. For parking and shuttle information, visit: pc.gc.ca/banffnow.

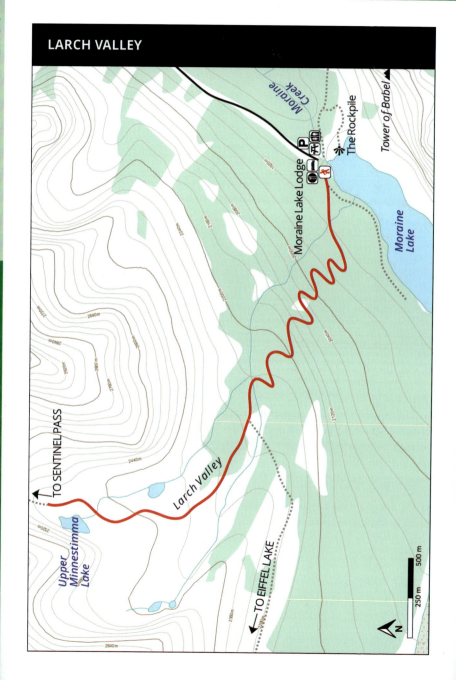

OPTION

Between the rugged walls of Pinnacle Mountain on the left and Mount Temple on the right, is the 2,611-metre summit of **SENTINEL PASS**. After passing the uppermost Minnestimma Lake, the trail begins a switchbacking climb of the steep, open slope leading to the pass—a vertical rise of nearly 200 metres that weeds out many Larch Valley hikers.

The sentinels of Sentinel Pass.

The rock formations surrounding Sentinel Pass lie nearly horizontal, and erosion of these layers has created the weird spires immediately north of the summit. The pass receives its name from these towers, the tallest of which is called the Grand Sentinel.

The pass was first ascended in 1894 by Samuel Allen and Yandell Henderson, members of a group of American mountain climbers exploring the Lake Louise region. A few days later they returned to the pass with their companions and climbed Mount Temple (3,544 metres), which was the first ascent in Canada above 11,000 feet.

Looking back to Larch Valley from the approach to Sentinel Pass.

Eiffel Lake

In 1894, before it was known as the Valley of the Ten Peaks, explorer Walter Wilcox and his companions named it Desolation Valley. In its deepest and most desolate heart is Eiffel Lake, reached by a high, contouring trail with continuous views of the peaks that have made the valley world famous.

Length: 5.6 km (3.5 miles) one way
Elevation gain: 410 metres (1,360 feet)
Allow: 1.5 to 2 hours one way
Rating: Moderate
Map: Gem Trek *Lake Louise & Yoho*

Trailhead N51°19.673′ W116°10.899′

Follow Moraine Lake Road 12.5 km to the parking area at Moraine Lake. Walk to the lakeshore and the trail sign below the lodge.

Trail Outline

- **0.0** Trailhead (elevation 1,887 metres).
  —Follow Moraine Lakeshore trail.
- **0.2** Junction. Eiffel Lake and Larch Valley right.
- **1.1** Switchbacks begin. Steady climb.
- **2.4** Junction. Larch Valley right. Eiffel Lake left.
  —Trail contours onto open slopes.
- **5.6** Eiffel Lake viewpoint (elevation 2,300 metres).

Trail Description

The Eiffel Lake trail follows the same course as the Larch Valley trail for the first 2.4 kilometres, switchbacking upward through closed forest from the north end of Moraine Lake. Splitting near the lower edge of Larch Valley, the Eiffel Lake trail continues along the north side of the Valley of the Ten Peaks. It soon emerges onto open slopes where all of the ten summits are revealed across the valley as well as the brilliant blue waters of Moraine Lake far below.

As the trail continues through flower-filled meadows, the Wenkchemna Glacier is barely discernible in the valley below. Heavy rockfall from the cliffs above the glacier has completely covered most of its surface, shielding the ice from the sun's rays and accounting in part for the glacier's relatively small recession over the past century.

The trail reaches Eiffel Lake and the best viewpoint on a steep scree slope well above its shores. Reflecting upon one of his first visits to the lake, Walter Wilcox wrote: "It would be difficult to find another lake of small size in a wilder setting, the

Beyond the Larch Valley junction, open spaces allow sweeping valley views.

shores being of great angular stones, perfectly in harmony with the wild range of mountains beyond. Except in one place where a green and inviting slope comes down to the water, this rough ground is utterly unsuitable for vegetation and nearly devoid of trees."

Eiffel Lake sits in the heart of an ancient rockslide.

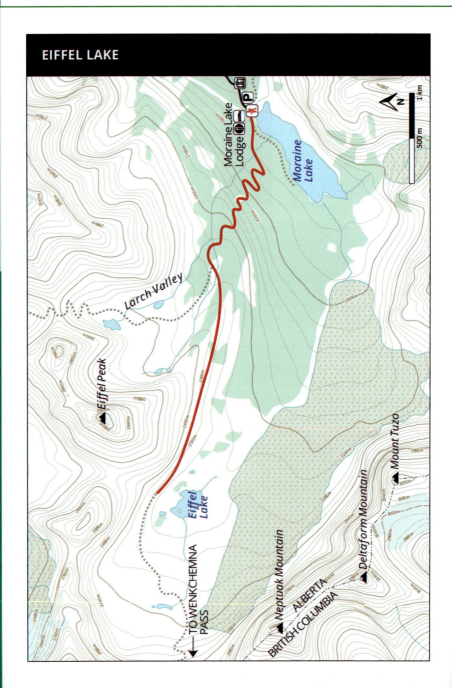

Eiffel's rugged surroundings were created by a massive rockslide that broke away from Neptuak Mountain in the distant past and spread rock debris across the valley. In fact, the lake undoubtedly formed after the slide, which created a natural dam for water flowing from the snowfields at the head of the valley. Immediately above the lake to the north is Eiffel Peak (3,085 metres), named for a rock pinnacle near its summit that resembles the famous Parisian tower.

If you don't want to labour down over 200 metres of broken rock to reach Eiffel Lake, you can enjoy an overview of both lake and the Ten Peaks by continuing west along the trail to a sheltering grove of larch trees—Wilcox's "green and inviting slope."

NOTES: Travel on the Eiffel Lake trail may require a group of four people hiking in close proximity to one another if special restrictions concerning grizzly bears are in place. These will be posted at the Lake Louise Visitor Centre and at the trailhead.

Moraine Lake Road is closed when the Moraine Lake parking area is full. This often happens as early as 7am, so plan on arriving early. For parking and shuttle information, visit: pc.gc.ca/banffnow.

OPTION

You can hike beyond Eiffel Lake for another four kilometres to **WENKCHEMNA PASS**, one of the highest trail-accessible points in the mountain national parks and an outstanding viewpoint for the Valley of the Ten Peaks. The trail continues due west across rolling alpine meadows, then climbs over moraine and along the rocky south ridge of Wenkchemna Peak before descending to the windswept gap between Wenkchemna Peak and Neptuak Mountain. (Sections of the trail may be obscured by snowfields before late July.)

Standing on the crest of the Continental Divide, you overlook the entire length of the Valley of the Ten Peaks. On the west side of the divide is the rocky Eagle's Eyrie region of Yoho National Park and, further south, the forested headwaters of Tokumm Creek in Kootenay National Park.

Descending from Wenkchemna Pass.

Consolation Lakes

The hike to Lower Consolation Lake is short and relatively flat, but the rugged scenery is as rewarding as that found on many of Banff's longer and more-demanding trails.

Length: 2.9 km (1.8 miles) one way
Elevation gain: 60 metres (195 feet)
Allow: 45 minutes one way
Rating: Easy
Map: Gem Trek *Lake Louise & Yoho*

Trailhead N51°19.703′ W116°10.872′

Follow Moraine Lake Road 12.5 km to the parking area at Moraine Lake. Walk down to the bridge over Moraine Creek, just below the lake outlet.

Trail Outline

- **0.0** Trailhead (elevation 1,885 metres).
- **0.1** Junction. Rockpile viewpoint right.
  —Cross avalanche slope and a gradual climb through forest begins.
- **2.3** Open meadow.
- **2.9** Lower Consolation Lake (elevation 1,945 metres).

Trail Description

After crossing the Moraine Creek bridge just below the parking area, the trail passes over a substantial rockslide, which is the natural dam that created Moraine Lake. A short trail branches to the top of **THE ROCKPILE**, where you are greeted by the classic view of Moraine Lake and the Valley of the Ten Peaks.

Beyond the rockslide, the trail enters a forest of spruce and fir and climbs gradually along the west side of Babel Creek. Just beyond the halfway point to the lake, the trail levels out along a meadow—a section that is often quite muddy.

A large rockslide blocks direct access to the north end of Lower Consolation Lake, but you still have a magnificent view of the lake and the glacier-capped summits of Bident and Quadra beyond. Mount Temple commands the view back down-valley to the north—at 3,544 metres, the third highest mountain in Banff National Park and the highest in the Lake Louise-Moraine Lake vicinity.

NOTES: Travel on the Consolation Lakes trail may require a group of four people hiking in close proximity to one another if special restrictions concerning grizzly bears are in place. These will be posted at the Lake Louise Visitor Centre and at the trailhead.

Moraine Lake Road is closed when the Moraine Lake parking area is full. This often happens as early as 7am, so plan on arriving early. For parking and shuttle information, visit: pc.gc.ca/banffnow.

Babel Creek flows beside the Consolation Lakes trail.

Lower Consolation Lake.

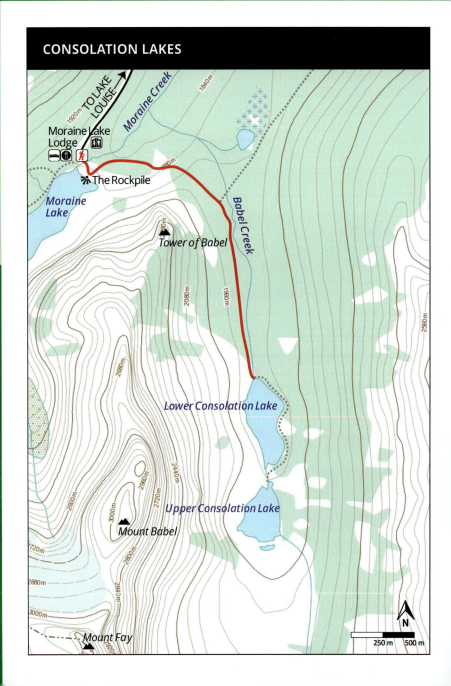

OPTION

If you are visiting Consolation after the high-water period (June to mid-July) and want to spend a little more time in the area, you can visit **UPPER CONSOLATION LAKE**. Cross Babel Creek below Lower Consolation Lake on rickety log booms and then follow a rough, muddy track along the lake's eastern shore. At the far end, climb over a ridge of rock debris separating the two lakes. (Good boots are required for this option.)

Detour to the Rockpile and you are greeted by this famous view.

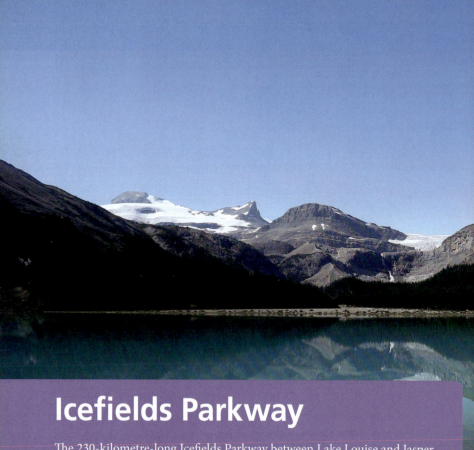

Icefields Parkway

The 230-kilometre-long Icefields Parkway between Lake Louise and Jasper is undeniably one of Canada's most scenic highways. More importantly for outdoor enthusiasts, it is the highest stretch of road in Canada, allowing hikers to reach the treeless alpine a lot quicker than elsewhere in the park, most notably at Bow Summit, Parker Ridge, and Wilcox Pass. Backcountry lakes, alpine meadows, and photogenic waterfalls add to the appeal for those planning on leaving the blacktop behind.

Bow Lake, along the Bow Glacier Falls trail.

Molar Pass

The Molar Pass trail is one of the longer and less-used routes detailed in this book. Aside from enjoying the solitude, the final destination is a high alpine pass with expansive wildflower meadows and expansive views.

Length: 10.5 km (6.5 miles) one way
Elevation gain: 510 metres (1,675 feet)
Allow: 3 hours one way
Rating: Moderate/difficul
Map: Gem Trek *Bow Lake & Saskatchewan Crossing*

Trailhead N51°37.801' W116°19.711'

Follow the Icefields Parkway north from the Trans-Canada Highway 24 km to Mosquito Creek Campground. The trail is across the highway from the campground entrance. (Trailhead parking on the west side of the road doubles as parking for Mosquito Creek Hostel).

Trail Outline

- **0.0** Trailhead (elevation 1,830 metres).
  —Short, steep climb followed by gradual uphill on rooty, rocky trail.
- **3.3** Side stream (bridged).
- **3.5** Side stream (bridged).
- **4.1** Major side stream (bridged).
- **5.0** Mosquito Creek Backcountry Campground.
- **5.1** Bridge to south side of Mosquito Creek.
- **6.8** Bridge to north side of Mosquito Creek.
- **7.4** Junction. North Molar Pass-Fish Lakes trail left. Molar Pass right.
  —Steady climb toward pass.
- **10.2** Trail crests Molar Pass meadows.
- **10.5** Molar Pass summit (elevation 2,340 metres).

Trail Description

Through its first seven kilometres, the Molar Pass trail rises gradually along open willow flats and subalpine forest near Mosquito Creek. The track is rocky and rooty most of the way, and there are numerous wet sections that can be particularly messy during wet summers or when a horse party has preceded you. Three small tributary streams (all bridged) are crossed in the first four kilometres.

Beyond the Mosquito Creek Backcountry Campground you immediately cross Mosquito Creek and then recross it 1.7 kilometres farther along. At km 7.4, you reach the junction where the North Molar Pass-Fish Lakes trail branches left from the Molar Pass trail. The Molar Pass trail is a bit indistinct over the next kilometre, and sections through open meadows are often waterlogged.

As the forest opens up, you get your first views of Molar Pass ahead. There are also numerous lush meadows sporting showy wildflowers, such as western anemone, globe flower, marsh marigold, purple fleabane, valerian, and ragwort.

Over the last two kilometres the trail climbs out of the trees and ascends across the valley's steep headwall to the crest of the pass. Another 300 metres of nearly flat, alpine meadow brings you to the true summit. The pass offers an excellent view of twin-peaked Molar Mountain (3,022 metres), rising above the meadows to the southeast. Farther off in that direction, across the Pipestone Valley, are the rugged peaks of the Slate Range, which contain the Skoki region. The glacier-crested summits of the Mount Hector massif rise immediately above the pass to the west and south.

The first half of the Molar Pass trail parallels Mosquito Creek.

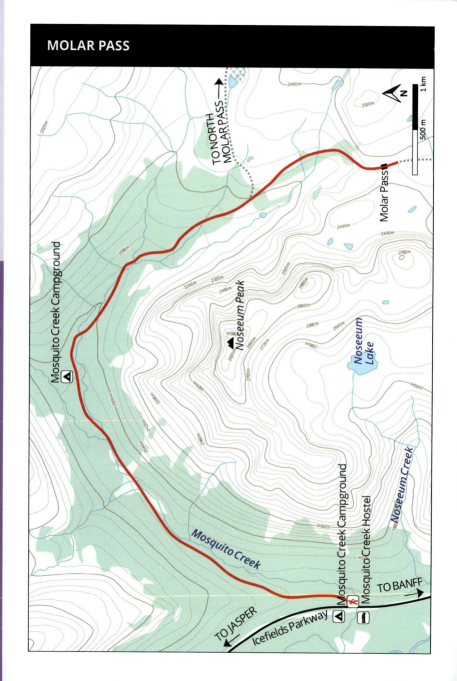

From Molar Pass, views extend north down the Mosquito Creek Valley (above) and south across alpine meadows to the Pipestone Valley (below).

Helen Lake

Wildflower meadows, lofty lakes and castellate peaks provide a constant change of scene that draws you onward to a remarkable, wide-open alpine landscape. Many consider this one of Banff National Park's best day hikes.

Length: 6 km (3.7 miles) one way
Elevation gain: 455 metres (1,490 feet)
Allow: 1.5 to 2 hours one way
Rating: Moderate
Map: Gem Trek *Bow Lake & Saskatchewan Crossing*

Trailhead N51°39.848' W116°26.307'

Follow the Icefields Parkway north from the Trans-Canada Highway 33 km to the Crowfoot Glacier Viewpoint. The short spur road to the Helen Lake trail parking area is on the opposite side of the highway from the viewpoint.

Trail Outline

- **0.0** Trailhead (elevation 1,950 metres).
  —Begin moderate to steep climb through subalpine forest.
- **2.4** Avalanche slope with open views.
- **2.9** Open views for remainder of hike.
- **3.4** Trail turns north at end of ridge.
  —Grade moderates into Helen Lake cirque.
- **4.5** Rockslide.
- **5.0** Helen Creek crossing.
- **6.0** Helen Lake (elevation 2,405 metres).

Trail Description

The Helen Lake trail climbs steadily through forest along the west-facing slopes of the Bow Valley for the first three kilometres and then emerges onto steep mountainside meadows. Views open across the valley to Crowfoot Mountain and Glacier, and the sharp summit of Mount Hector (3,394 metres), down-valley to the southeast.

The trail reaches the south end of a long ridge at kilometre 3.4, where a scattering of whitebark pine indicate that you are nearing treeline. Here it

Wildflowers are a colourful highlight of the Helen Lake trail (above) while the lake itself is a scenic gem (below).

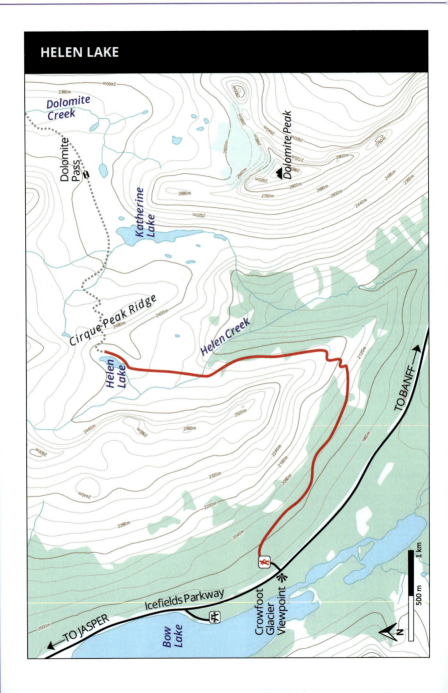

switches around 90 degrees and contours into the amphitheatre containing Helen Lake.

After another kilometre of gradual ascent through lightly forested meadows, you drop beneath the toe of a relatively recent rockslide. The pile of tumbled boulders is surrounded by a lush snowbed plant community filled with the colourful blooms of purple fleabane, paintbrush, ragwort and valerian. Beyond the slide the trail climbs above the last trees and remains above treeline for the rest of the hike.

Helen Lake is bordered by open alpine meadows and scree slopes beneath the summit of Cirque Peak. It is a great place to kick-back and enjoy the scene, which is home to an amazing number of hoary marmots, who seem to have nothing better to do than sit in the sun and count passing hikers.

OPTION

Helen Lake would be an above average destination on most hikes, but you shouldn't end your day there. Gather your strength and continue for at least another 900 metres up a steep series of switchbacks to **CIRQUE PEAK RIDGE**. The 2,500-metre-high ridge, extending south from Cirque Peak, is the highest point on the trail, and it provides an outstanding overview of Katherine Lake and Dolomite Pass to the east and Helen

Helen Lake from Cirque Peak Ridge.

Lake and its meadows back to the southwest. However, do take care on these exposed heights. When the weather is deteriorating in the Bow Valley, it is absolutely vile on this windswept ridge.

For most day hikers the ridge is a good spot to turn for home, but if you don't mind climbing back over this ridge at the end of the day, you can descend to **KATHERINE LAKE** and **DOLOMITE PASS**. The trail drops nearly 100 metres to the north end of Katherine Lake, which stretches beneath the castellate cliffs of Dolomite Peak. An opening beyond the south end of the lake serves as a window to the southern half of Banff National Park, and on a clear day the sharp horn of Mount Assiniboine is visible 100 kilometres away. Though the trail is not well defined beyond Katherine Lake, it is an easy climb over spongy alpine meadows to a small lake on the crest of Dolomite Pass. Dolomite Pass lies three kilometres beyond Helen Lake, so the roundtrip to the pass will create a very full 18-kilometre day.

Bow Glacier Falls

The Bow Glacier basin has been a popular half-day trip for travellers ever since the tourist-explorer Walter Wilcox visited it in 1896. The glacier, which filled much of the basin in Wilcox's day, has retreated above the headwall, leaving a 120-metre-high waterfall as the only hint of the icefield hidden above.

Length: 4.7 km (2.9 miles) one way
Elevation gain: 95 metres (310 feet)
Allow: 1.5 hours one way
Rating: Easy/moderate
Map: Gem Trek *Bow Lake & Saskatchewan Crossing*

Trailhead N51°40.727′ W116°27.886′

Follow the Icefields Parkway north from the Trans-Canada Highway 36 km to the Num-Ti-Jah Lodge access road at Bow Lake. Follow the access road 400 metres to the public parking area and washrooms.

Trail Outline

0.0	Trailhead (elevation 1,960 metres).
	—Follow shoreline trail to lodge parking lot.
0.3	Trail sign at lodge parking lot.
	—Trail follows Bow Lake shoreline.
1.9	Bow Lake inlet. Trail follows along stream.
2.7	Broad gravel flats.
3.4	Bottom of canyon. Steep uphill along canyon.
3.6	Bow Glacier basin viewpoint.
	—Trail continues across basin to falls.
4.7	Bow Glacier Falls (elevation 2,055 metres).

Trail Description

A broad pathway skirts along Bow Lake from the trailhead parking area to a secondary trailhead just beyond the lodge parking lot. From there, it launches off across willow flats to the lake's northern shoreline. A more modest track, often muddy and sometimes flooded in spots, follows along the lake to the alluvial flats at its inlet. Views along this section include Crowfoot Mountain

The first section of trail follows the shoreline of Bow Lake.

across the lake and the leaning spire of Mount St. Nicholas rising from the white expanse of the Wapta Glacier on the skyline ahead.

The route beyond the lake is mainly flat, with an occasional brief climb, and follows near the silty, glacier-fed steam draining the basin. At 3.4 kilometres you reach a narrow canyon and make a short, steep climb along its rim (this section is hazardous when wet, icy or snow-covered). As described by Wilcox: "Where the canyon is deepest an immense block of limestone about twenty-five feet long has fallen down, and with either end resting on the canyon walls, it affords a natural bridge over the gloomy chasm."

The trail does not cross the natural bridge, but continues up along the gorge to the sparsely-forested crest of a terminal moraine. From this viewpoint the glacial basin lies beneath you, and Bow Glacier Falls pours off the headwall beyond.

You can continue another 1.1 kilometres across the rocky basin to the base of the falls, which is fed by a small meltwater lake near the toe of the Bow Glacier. The waterfall is most impressive during the warmest days of summer.

Bow Glacier Falls.

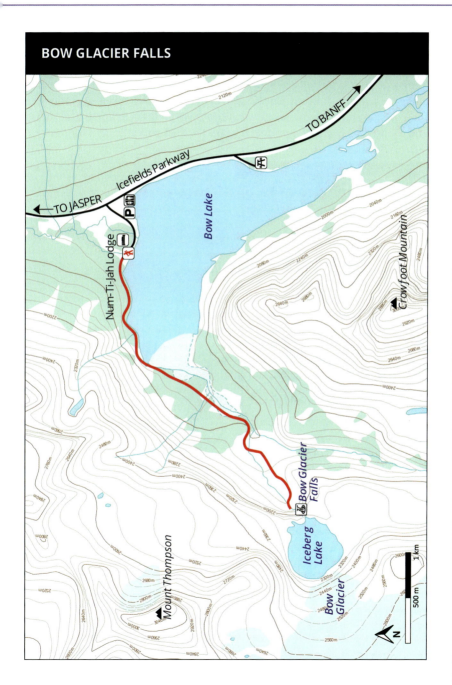

Bow Summit Lookout

The paved trail to Peyto Lake viewpoint is one of the most popular short walks along the Icefields Parkway. But you can continue beyond this busy overlook to the Bow Summit fire lookout site, where you will find peace, alpine meadows, and a lofty view overlooking Bow Summit, the Mistaya Valley, and Bow Lake.

Length: 3.1 km (1.9 miles) one way
Elevation gain: 230 metres (760 feet)
Allow: 1 hour one way
Rating: Moderate
Map: Gem Trek *Bow Lake & Saskatchewan Crossing*

Trailhead N51°43.022′ W116°29.982′

Follow the Icefields Parkway north from the Trans-Canada Highway for 41 km to Bow Summit and the Peyto Lake parking area.

Trail Outline

- 0.0 Trailhead (elevation 2,085 metres).
- 0.6 Peyto Lake Viewpoint.
  —Follow paved trail uphill (right-hand option).
- 0.7 Junction. Follow middle trail angling uphill to left.
- 0.9 Follow old roadbed ahead.
- 2.4 Descend into basin.
- 2.6 Stream crossing.
- 3.1 Bow Summit Lookout (elevation 2,315 metres).

Trail Description

Follow the paved nature trail uphill from the Peyto Lake parking area to the viewing platform overlooking Peyto Lake. Take the obligatory photo, then escape on the right-hand of two paved trails leading uphill. Within 100 metres you arrive at a three-way junction at an interpretive sign. Continue on the middle branch angling uphill to the left of the sign—an arm of the upper Bow Summit nature trail loop. In a few minutes the paved trail turns right, but you continue straight ahead on the remains of the old fire lookout service road.

The Bow Summit Lookout trail passes this famous lookout above Peyto Lake.

The roadbed soon switchbacks over a rise with views back to Peyto Lake. From this rise, the trail turns southeast and climbs steadily along the mountain slope. Views over Bow Summit continue to improve throughout the ascent. As you climb, you enter the *kruppelholz* zone—an area where islands of altitude-stunted alpine fir dwindle into treeless alpine meadow.

Wildflowers bloom in profusion throughout this section in July and August, dominated by white-flowered valerian and white, pink and magenta varieties of Indian paintbrush. Higher up the lush growth

The Bow Summit Lookout trail is a reliable place to see marmots.

is replaced by fields of ground-hugging white mountain avens, and white and pink mountain heather.

At kilometre 2.4, the trail drops into a draw and crosses a small stream beneath a huge rockslide. We call this Marmot Basin, since we have often encountered curious hoary marmots bounding along the stream and sunning themselves on the nearby boulders. The stream is bordered with moisture-loving flowers, including yellow ragwort and red-stemmed saxifrage.

Mistaya Valley from Bow Summit Lookout.

The roadbed climbs steeply beside a great mound of rock rubble over the final 500 metres to the alpine knoll where the Bow Summit fire lookout cabin once stood. Until it was removed in the 1970s, it was the highest fire lookout in Banff National Park.

From the old lookout site you have open views of the Icefields Parkway crossing Bow Summit and the entire Mistaya Valley, including Waterfowl Lakes, to the north. By following a steep footpath for another 200 metres

BOW SUMMIT LOOKOUT

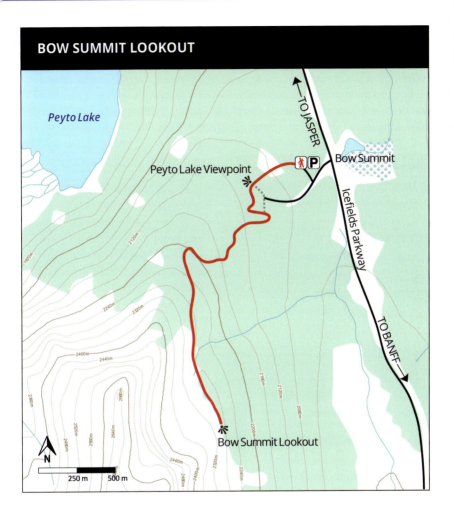

beyond the knoll, you reach the best viewpoint for Bow Lake and the glaciated peaks to the south.

The mountain rising directly above you is Mount Jimmy Simpson, named for the pioneer guide and outfitter who began the development of Num-Ti-Jah Lodge on the shores of Bow Lake in 1922. He lived there until his death in 1972 at age 95.

Chephren Lake

While you can admire the rugged pinnacles of Mount Chephren and Howse Peak from the roadside pullout beside Lower Waterfowl Lake, the mountains are best seen from the shores of Chephren Lake, which lies at the very foot of the escarpment.

Length: 3.5 km (2.2 miles) one way
Elevation gain: 105 metres (345 feet)
Allow: 1 hour one way
Rating: Easy
Map: Gem Trek *Bow Lake & Saskatchewan Crossing*

Trailhead N51°50.448′ W116°37.393′

Follow the Icefields Parkway north from the Trans-Canada Highway for 57 km to Waterfowl Lakes Campground. On the campground access road, continue straight ahead (beyond campground entrance). A 400-metre trail leads to the trailhead at the Mistaya River bridge, which is also accessible from the campground.

Trail Outline

- **0.0** Trailhead (elevation 1,650 metres). —Moderate uphill into subalpine forest.
- **1.3** Junction. Cirque Lake left; Chephren Lake right.
- **1.6** Meadow to left of trail.
- **3.5** Chephren Lake (elevation 1,713 metres).

Trail Description

The Chephren Lake hike begins at the Mistaya River footbridge at the rear of Waterfowl Lakes Campground. After crossing

The bridge across the Mistaya River.

Chephren Lake.

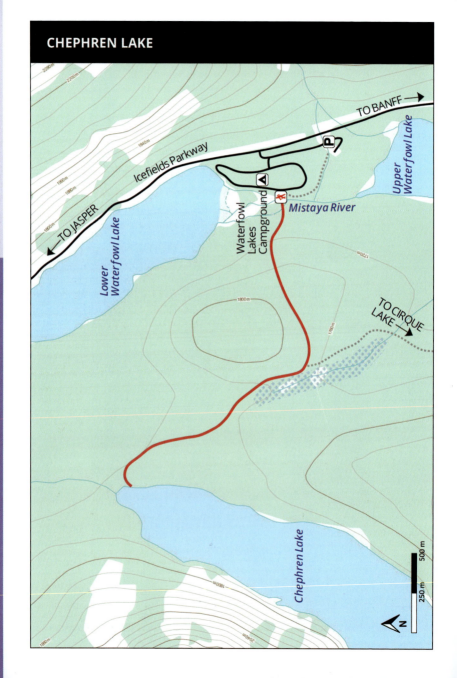

the Mistaya bridge, you climb quickly through forest to a trail junction. Chephren Lake, the most popular destination, is to the right, Cirque Lake to the left. There is little gain or loss of elevation from the junction to Chephren Lake, but the trail is often a muddy mess. Views en route are limited to a brief glimpse of Howse Peak at a trailside meadow.

Two great peaks rise above Chephren Lake: the imposing, glaciated mountain to the south is Howse Peak, site of frequent avalanches in spring and early summer; Mount Chephren (pronounced kefren) forms the west shore and is named for the second-largest of the three great pyramids of Egypt.

OPTION

Because it is a bit smaller and the approach a bit longer and steeper, **CIRQUE LAKE** is less frequently visited than Chephren. From the 1.3-kilometre junction, take the left fork for Cirque Lake. The trail descends gradually to Cirque Lake's outlet stream then climbs beside it through heavy subalpine forest to the lake—a distance of 2.9 kilometres from the junction. Midway, Stairway and Aries Peaks create the 800-metre-high wall rising beyond its far shore. If you visit both lakes on your trip, the total roundtrip distance is 12.8 kilometres.

Cirque Lake.

Nigel Pass

Nigel Pass is one of the most rewarding day trips in the Columbia Icefield vicinity. Atop this open, rocky ridge on the boundary of Banff and Jasper National Parks, there are expansive views back to rugged, glaciated peaks near the Icefield and north into Jasper's remote Brazeau River Valley.

Length: 7.4 km (4.6 miles) one way
Elevation gain: 335 metres (1,100 feet)
Allow: 2 to 2.5 hours one way
Rating: Moderate
Map: Gem Trek *Columbia Icefield*

Trailhead N52°11.250' W117°04.227'

Follow the Icefields Parkway north from the Trans-Canada Highway for 114 km to the Nigel Creek parking area. The parking area is above a barrier gate below the highway.

Trail Outline

0.0	Trailhead (elevation 1,860 metres).
	—Follow gravel road.
2.0	Patrol cabin.
2.2	Creek crossings and equestrian trail to left.
2.3	Camp Parker.
2.4	Trail begins ascent along east side of Nigel Creek Valley.
5.3	Trail enters open meadows.
	—Begin ascent to park boundary.
7.4	Nigel Pass (elevation 2,195 metres).

Trail Description

Follow a service road from the barrier gate for two kilometres to a patrol cabin and look for the trail descending into the forest just beyond. Upon reaching Hilda Creek, there's a bridged crossing, following immediately by another, over Nigel Creek.

At kilometre 2.3 the site of old Camp Parker is passed in a stand of large Engelmann spruce. This area was used as a campsite by indigenous hunters before the arrival of Europeans, and mountaineers exploring the Columbia Icefield region at the turn of the 20th century continued the tradition.

The carvings on the surrounding trees record the visits of many of these early campers, though most date to the period following the opening of the Icefields Parkway in 1940.

At Camp Parker the trail turns north and begins the ascent to Nigel Creek's headwaters. Throughout this section there are good views back to Parker Ridge and Hilda Peak—a sharp sub-peak of Mount Athabasca. Nigel Pass is seldom out-of-sight ahead.

The trail climbs more seriously over the last kilometre to the trail summit, attained on a rocky ridge that marks the boundary between Banff and Jasper National Parks. (The true summit of Nigel Pass lies just over a kilometre to the northeast.)

Forest cover is very sparse and stunted on this 2,195-metre-high ridge, an indication of the upper limit of tree growth in this latitude. Back down-valley to the south, the ice-clad summit of Mount Saskatchewan (3,342 metres) rises beyond Parker Ridge. To the north is the wild Brazeau River Valley and the maze of peaks comprising the southern region of Jasper National Park. Directly west of the pass, rising above a large cirque, is Nigel Peak, named in 1898 by British mountaineers Hugh Stutfield and Norman Collie for their packer Nigel Vavasour.

The creek crossing at km 2.2 is a good place to appreciate two different water sources—the glacially-fed Hilda Creek from the west and the clear snowmelt water of Nigel Creek from the north.

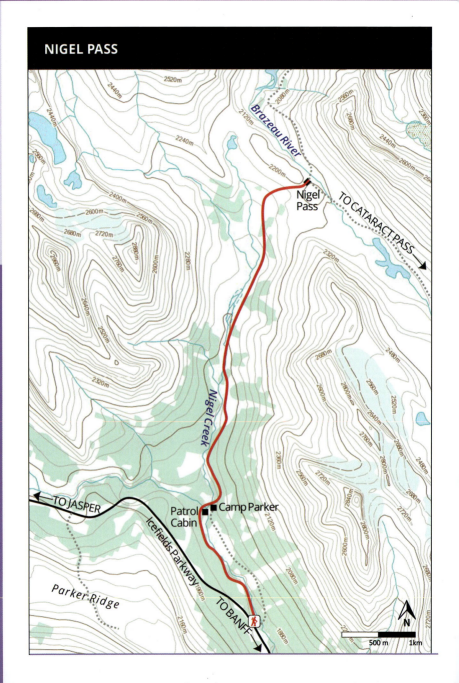

Looking west to Nigel Peak from the summit of the Nigel Pass trail.

OPTION

A 100-metre descent from Nigel Pass brings you to the south fork of the Brazeau River (an easy rock-hop crossing). Continue northwest (to the left) for a kilometre or so where there are even better views of the **BRAZEAU RIVER VALLEY** and back to the north side of Nigel Pass—a fine rock wall featuring several small waterfalls.

After descending and crossing the Brazeau River from Nigel Pass, another trail heads off upstream, to the right. This lightly travelled route eventually leads six kilometres to remote **CATARACT PASS**, at the headwaters of the south fork of the Brazeau River. While no maintained trail leads in this direction, energetic explorers can pick a route through the open terrain and then over a boulder field before descending to expansive meadows and a string of milky-turquoise ponds that begin just over one kilometre from the Brazeau River crossing.

Milky turquoise ponds and alpine meadows make travel beyond Nigel Pass a worthwhile option.

Parker Ridge

Parker Ridge is a short, wonderful excursion into the alpine life zone. The northernmost trail in Banff National Park passes through lush wildflower meadows and quickly climbs above the treeline to a high, open ridge with a spectacular view of the Saskatchewan Glacier.

Length: 2.7 km (1.7 miles) one way
Elevation gain: 250 metres (820 feet)
Allow: 1 hour one way
Rating: Moderate
Map: Gem Trek *Columbia Icefield*

Trailhead N52°11.491′ W117°06.943′

Follow the Icefields Parkway 118 km north of the Trans-Canada highway or four km south of Sunwapta Pass to the Parker Ridge trailhead parking area.

Trail Outline

0.0	Trailhead (elevation 2,000 metres).
	—Steady switchbacking ascent.
1.1	Trail emerges onto open alpine slopes. Switchbacks continue.
2.1	Parker Ridge summit (elevation 2,250 metres).
	—Trail contours along ridge to southeast (left).
2.5	First Saskatchewan Glacier viewpoint.
2.7	Second Saskatchewan Glacier viewpoint.

Trail Description

The lower section of the Parker Ridge trail switchbacks steadily upward through scattered stands of alpine fir and open meadows created by snowslides. Wildflowers in this section are protected from the elements and nourished by abundant moisture from snowmelt. Tall, showy flowers, like paintbrush, valerian, purple fleabane, and fringed grass-of-Parnassus, bloom from early July through mid-August.

Halfway up the north-facing slope, at an elevation of 2,100 metres, you emerge above treeline into the alpine zone—a region of tiny ground-hugging plants. In this harsh, wind-scoured environment the blooms of moss campion, white mountain avens, rock jasmine, and forget-me-nots last only a couple of weeks.

After passing above an extensive talus slope (domain of pikas), the trail makes its final switchbacking ascent to the 2,250-metre-high crest of the ridge. From this summit it veers left and makes a slight descent to the first of two viewpoints for the nine-kilometre-long Saskatchewan Glacier.

While many hikers stop at the first viewpoint, another 200 metres farther along provides the most rewarding prospect of the glacier and the uppermost limits of the North Saskatchewan River. A rocky promontory at the viewpoint is filled with fossil coral and covered by orange foliose (*Xanthoria*) lichen.

The ridgetop is also a rich area for alpine wildlife and birds. It is frequently visited by both bighorn sheep and mountain goats, and occasionally a grizzly bear wanders through. Rosy finches and horned larks nest here in summer, white-tailed ptarmigan are year-round residents, and golden eagles and hawks patrol the meadows around the glacier viewpoints for Columbian ground squirrels.

NOTES: The Parker Ridge trail was built in the 1960s, and it was designed with a series of gradually ascending switchbacks. Unfortunately, this encouraged people to shortcut straight downhill on their return from the summit. A number of barriers and "official" shortcuts (staircases) were constructed to discourage this slope-damaging practice. Be considerate

After passing through this short stretch of subalpine forest near the trailhead, the Parker Ridge trail rises above the treeline.

This sign marks the high point of the Parker Ridge trail.

Saskatchewan Glacier from Parker Ridge.

of this fragile, easily eroded environment and stay on the designated trail or staircases.

Because the trail ascends a north-facing slope, snowbanks often cover the route into early July. To help preserve the fragile meadows, Parks Canada usually keeps the area closed until the track is snow-free. You should check on the trail's status at a park visitor centre if you plan on hiking it before mid-July.

PARKER RIDGE

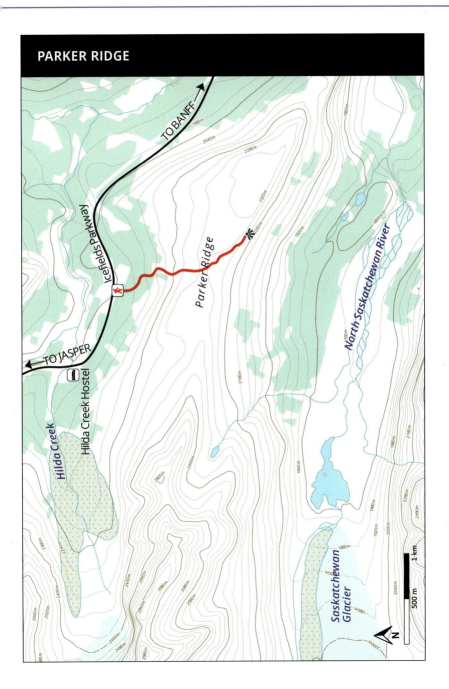

Wilcox Pass

Just across the boundary of Jasper National Park, we've included Wilcox Pass in this book as it is one of the finest day hikes along the Icefields Parkway. The trail leads high above the treeline and into an alpine valley high above the Columbia Icefield.

Length: 4 km (2.5 miles) one way
Elevation gain: 335 metres (1,100 feet)
Allow: 1.5 hours one way
Rating: Moderate
Map: Gem Trek *Columbia Icefield*

Trailhead N52°13.098′ W117°11.104′

Trailhead parking is on the access road to Wilcox Creek Campground, along the Icefields Parkway 124 km north of the Trans-Canada Highway and three km south of the Glacier Discovery Centre.

Trail Outline

- **0.0** Trailhead (elevation 2,040 metres).
  —Moderately steep climb through subalpine forest.
- **1.8** Trail emerges above treeline.
  —Grade moderates.
- **2.5** Athabasca Glacier viewpoint.
  —Short, steep climb to alpine meadows.
- **4.0** Wilcox Pass Summit (elevation 2,375 metres).

Trail Description

From the entrance to Wilcox Creek Campground, Canada's highest roadside campground, the trail climbs directly through a mature subalpine forest. This initial stretch is steep, gaining 120 metres of elevation in less than a kilometre.

The grade moderates as you break out of the trees and emerge onto an open ridge overlooking the Icefields Parkway and the Athabasca Glacier. The Rockies' most famous valley glacier is the centrepiece of an exceptional panorama, which includes such ice-covered giants as Mount Athabasca (3,491 metres), Snow Dome (3,460 metres), and Mount Kitchener (3,511 metres).

The view east from the Wilcox Pass trail toward Cirrus Mountain.

Beyond the viewpoint, the trail climbs steeply along the edge of a gully containing a small stream. After this short, stiff ascent, it levels out across alpine tundra and heads northwest into the long U-shaped pass between Wilcox and Nigel Peaks. Here, in mid-summer (late July to mid-August), the lush, tall wildflowers of treeline are replaced by ground-hugging alpine plants, like forget-me-not, white mountain avens, and moss campion.

As soon as you reach the summit meadows, scan the nearby slopes and ridges for bighorn sheep. Mature rams hang together here each summer, leaving flocks of ewes, lambs and immature

Looking toward Wilcox Peak from the pass.

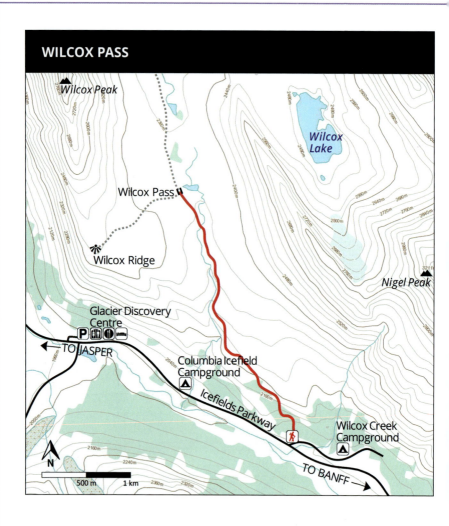

males to feed in the valley below. Wilcox Pass is one of the most reliable places in the Canadian Rockies to see bighorns at close range in a backcountry setting.

The official summit of Wilcox Pass is reached four kilometres from the trailhead, though the pass is so long and flat it is difficult to recognize it as the highest point. (A large rock cairn beside the trail marks the spot.) Wilcox Peak dominates the view looking up valley, while the heavily-glaciated north face of Mount Athabasca is visible back across the meadows to the south.

Wilcox Peak and Pass are named for American mountaineer Walter Wilcox, whose horseback party first crossed the pass in 1896. The pass became the standard route north following Wilcox's trip since it avoided the rugged Sunwapta Gorge and the Athabasca Glacier, which, at that time, nearly blocked the valley below.

> **OPTION**
>
> Although you can continue northwest through Wilcox Pass as far as Tangle Falls on the Icefields Parkway, our favourite side-trip is the 1.4-kilometre trail running southwest to **WILCOX RIDGE** (signposted from the pass). This ridge, just south of Wilcox Peak, offers an amazing aerial viewpoint overlooking the Athabasca Glacier.

Looking down to the Athabasca Glacier from Wilcox Ridge.

Index

Abbot Pass 131
Abbot Pass Hut 131
Abbot Pass Viewpoint 131
Allen, Samuel 145
Alpine Club of Canada 116, 131, 139
Arnica Lake 9, 111, 112, 113
Arnica Lake trail 9, **111-113**
Arnica Summit 113
Athabasca Glacier 11, 184, 187
Aylmer Lookout 58
Aylmer Pass 58

Babel Creek 153
Ball Pass 110
Banff & Lake Louise Tourism 23
Banff Avenue 60
Banff Gondola 34, 42, 43, 44
Banff Railway Station 20
Banff Springs Golf Course 28
Banff Springs Hotel (see *Fairmont Banff Springs*)
Banff, town of 4, 5, 7, 12, 26, 28, 30, 32, 44, 60, 68, 80, 132
Banff Visitor Centre 22, 58
Bankhead 53, 54
Barrymore, John 134
bears 14-15, 58, 91, 139, 142, 149, 151, 181
beavers 17
Bident Mountain 114, 150
Big Beehive 122, 126, 128
bighorn sheep 181, 185, 186
Boom Creek 114
Boom Lake 114, 116
Boom Lake trail **114-116**
Boom Mountain 114, 116
Bourgeau Base Area 84, 100
Bourgeau Lake 104, 105, 106
Bourgeau Lake trail **104-107**
Bow Glacier 165
Bow Glacier Falls 164, 165, 166
Bow Glacier Falls trail 154, **164-167**
Bow Lake 154-155, 164, 165, 168, 171
Bow River 5, 31, 32, 35, 38, 47, 48
Bow Summit 154, 168, 170
Bow Summit Lookout 168
Bow Summit Lookout trail **168-171**
Bow Valley 12, 28, 29, 30, 60, 68, 76, 80, 81, 83, 104, 113, 117, 127, 132, 160, 163
Bow Valley Parkway 4, 67, 68, 72, 76, 79
Brazeau River 179
Brazeau River Valley 176, 177, 179
Brewster Creek 46, 48

Brewster Rock 92
British Columbia 18, 87, 92, 96, 99

C Level Cirque 53, 54, 55
C Level Cirque trail **53-55**
Calgary International Airport 5, 18
Camp Parker 176-177
Camp, Walter 73
camping 21-22
Canadian Pacific Railway (CPR) 76, 83, 129, 131
Canmore 28, 55, 60
Carver, Billy 50
Cascade Amphitheatre 63, 64
Cascade Amphitheatre trail **63-65**
Cascade Mountain 44, 50, 53, 54, 55, 60, 62, 63, 64, 76, 77
Castle Junction 76, 111, 114
Castle Lookout 80, 81, 83
Castle Lookout trail **80-83**
Castle Mountain 67
Castle Mountain Chalets 76
Castle Mountain Syncline 77
Cataract Pass 179
Cave and Basin National Historic Site 46, 47, 48
Central Gully 39, 40
Chateau Lake Louise 122, 128, 132
Chephren Lake 172, 173, 175
Chephren Lake trail **172-175**
Cirque Lake 172, 175
Cirque Peak 1634
Cirque Peak Ridge 163
Cirrus Mountain 187
Citadel Lake 96
Citadel Pass 8, 84, 86, 90, 92, 96, 97, 99
Citadel Pass trail 84, 86, 87, **96-99**
Citadel Peak 90, 97
Collie, Norman 177
Columbia Icefield 5, 11, 23, 176, 184
Consolation Lakes 15, 150, 151, 153
Consolation Lakes trail **150-153**
Consolation Valley 119
Continental Divide 5, 8, 84, 86, 96, 97, 99, 100, 108, 149
Copper Mountain 76
Cory Pass 68, 69, 71
Cory Pass trail **68-71**
Cosmic Ray Station 44
Crowfoot Glacier 160
Crowfoot Glacier Viewpoint 160
Crowfoot Mountain 160, 164

Devil's Gap 58
Devil's Thumb 126
Dolomite Pass 163
Dolomite Peak 163
Eagle's Eyrie 149
Edith Pass trail 71
Egypt Lake 103
Eiffel Lake 15, 146, 147, 149
Eiffel Lake trail 142, **146-149**
Eiffel Peak 149
Eisenhower Tower 76, 77
elk 15, 31, 32
Elk Lake trail 63, 64
Eohippus Lake 103
Eternal Love 134

Fairholme Range 54, 57
Fairmont Banff Springs 28, 34, 35, 36
Fairview Lookout 132
Fairview Mountain 132, 135
Fatigue Mountain 97
Fatigue Pass 99
Fireside Picnic Area 68
Forty Mile Creek 63, 64
Forty Mile Creek Valley 71
Front Ranges 56

Gargoyle Valley 71
Gem Trek maps 23
Giant Steps 136, 139, 140-141
giardia 17, 25
Gibbon Pass 108, 110
Glacier Discovery Centre 23, 184
gondola 8, 42, 43, 44, 84, 100
Grand Sentinel 145
grizzly bears 14-15, 139, 142, 149, 151, 181
Grizzly Lake 8, 86, 87, 90

Harvey Lake 107
Harvey Pass 107
Harvey, Ralph 107
Healy Creek 100, 103
Healy Creek Campground 100
Healy Meadows 103
Healy Pass 13, 92, 100, 101, 103
Healy Pass trail **100-103**
Hector, Dr. James 106
Helen Creek 160
Helen Lake 10, 160, 161, 163
Helen Lake trail 10, **160-163**
Helena Ridge 76, 78
Henderson, Yandell 145
Highline trail 122, 128
Highway 93 South 4, 18, 83
Hilda Creek 176
Hilda Peak 177
Hoodoos trail 20, **31-33**

Hoodoos Viewpoint 31
Horn, Camilla 134
Horseshoe Glacier 139
Horseshoe Meadows 136, 139
Howard Douglas Lake 96, 97, 99
Howse Peak 172, 175
Hungabee Mountain 139

Icefields Parkway 4, 5, 6, 17, 18, 154, 156, 160, 164, 168, 176, 180, 184
Ink Pots 74

Jasper National Park 4, 18, 77, 176, 177
Johnson Lake 50, 51, 52
Johnson Lake trail **50-52**
Johnston Canyon 8, 20, 67, 72, 75
Johnston Canyon Campground 22, 75
Johnston Canyon Resort 72, 73
Johnston Canyon trail **72-75**
Johnston Creek 72, 74

Kain, Conrad 69
Kananaskis Country 5
Katherine Lake 163
Kootenay National Park 5, 18, 87, 91, 149

Lake Agnes 9, 120, 122, 123, 124, 125, 126
Lake Agnes Tea House 122, 125
Lake Agnes-Plain of the Six Glaciers Circuit 126
Lake Agnes trail 9, **122-127**, 128
Lake Annette 133, 136, 137, 139
Lake Louise 4, 5, 6, 9, 10, 12, 20, 67, 81, 83, 117, 120, 122, 125, 128, 129, 131, 132, 134, 135
Lake Louise Campground 22
Lake Louise Lakeshore trail 128
Lake Louise overflow parking 20, 21
Lake Louise, village of 23, 136
Lake Louise Visitor Centre 22, 23, 139, 143, 149, 151
Lake Minnewanka 7, 20, 44, 53, 54, 56, 57, 58
Lake Minnewanka Road 20, 50, 53, 56
Lake Minnewanka trail 15, **56-59**
larch 77, 89, 100, 101, 103, 112, 119, 126, 132, 142
Larch Valley 10, 15, 120, 132, 142, 143, 145, 146, 147
Larch Valley trail 10, 139, **142-145**, 146
Larix Lake 8, 86, 88, 89, 90
Little Beehive 122, 126
Lookout Mountain 92
loons 51
Lost Horse Creek Campground 108
Lower Consolation Lake 150, 151, 153
Lower Falls 72, 73, 74
Lower Twin Lake 113
Lower Waterfowl Lake 172

INDEX

Marguerite Falls 72, 73
marmots 10, 63, 104, 129, 169, 170
Marsh Loop 46, 48
Massive Range 29, 48, 103, 104
McCarthy, Albert 69
Meadow Park 90, 92, 103
Minnestimma Lakes 142
Mirror Lake 122, 123, 126, 128
Mistaya River 172
Mistaya Valley 168, 170
Mitre Col 136
Molar Mountain 157
Molar Pass 156, 157, 159
Molar Pass trail **156-159**
Monarch Ramparts 84, 92, 103
Monarch, The 92, 103
Monarch Viewpoint 66-67, 90, 92, 103
Moraine Creek 150
Moraine Lake 6, 15, 20-21, 83, 119, 120, 139, 142, 146, 149, 150, 151
Moraine Lake Road 21, 136, 139, 142, 143, 146, 149, 150, 151
Moraine Lakeshore trail 142, 146
Mosquito Creek 156, 157
Mosquito Creek Campground 156
Mosquito Creek Hostel 156
Mosquito Creek Valley 159
Mount Assiniboine 87, 90, 92, 96, 99, 100, 103, 107
Mount Assiniboine Provincial Park 5, 87, 99
Mount Athabasca 11, 177, 184, 186
Mount Aylmer 58
Mount Ball 108, 110
Mount Bell 119
Mount Bourgeau 29, 103, 104, 105, 107
Mount Brett 103, 104, 107
Mount Chephren 172, 175
Mount Cory 69
Mount Edith 47, 64, 69, 71
Mount Eisenhower Fire Lookout 81)
Mount Girouard 58
Mount Hector 132, 157, 160
Mount Inglismaldie 54, 58
Mount Jimmy Simpson 171
Mount Kitchener 184
Mount Lefroy 128, 129, 131
Mount Louis 64, 68, 69, 71
Mount Niblock 125
Mount Norquay 35, 60
Mount Norquay ski area 60, 63, 64
Mount Rundle 28, 32, 38, 40, 50, 55, 60
Mount Rundle trail **38-41**
Mount Rundle Backcountry Campground 34
Mount Saskatchewan 177
Mount St. Nicholas 165
Mount Temple 81, 83, 132, 133, 135, 136, 137, 139, 145, 150

Mount Victoria 128, 129, 131, 135
Mount Whyte 125
mountain goats 181
Mystic Pass 63

Neptuak Mountain 149
Nigel Creek 176, 177
Nigel Pass 176, 177, 179
Nigel Pass trail, **176-179**
Nigel Peak 177, 179, 185
North Molar Pass-Fish Lakes trail 156, 157
North Saskatchewan River 5, 181
Num-Ti-Jah Lodge 164, 171

O'Brien Lake 117, 119
Old Quarry Loop 34, 36

Palliser Expedition 106
Palliser Range 54
Panorama Ridge 119
Panorama Ridge Meadows 119
Paradise Creek 136, 137, 139
Paradise Valley 10, 15, 133, 136, 137, 139
Paradise Valley Campground 136, 139
Paradise Valley trail 10, **136-141**
Parker Ridge 11, 154, 177, 180, 181, 182
Parker Ridge trail 11, **180-183**
Parks Canada 21, 22, 131, 182
Parks Canada Campground Reservation Service 22
Peter Lougheed Provincial Park 5
Peyto Lake 168, 169
Peyto Lake Viewpoint 168
Pharaoh Creek 108
Pharaoh Creek junction 108
Pharaoh Peaks 103
pikas 63, 104, 107, 129, 181
Pilot Mountain 76, 83
Pinnacle Mountain 145
Pipestone Valley 157, 159
Plain of the Six Glaciers Tea House 126, 128, 129
Plain of the Six Glaciers trail 9, 126, **128-131**
ptarmigan 104, 107

Quadra Mountain 114, 150
Quartz Hill 90, 96, 97, 99

Redearth Creek 108
Ringrose Peak 139
Roam Transit buses 19, 20, 32
Rock Isle-Grizzly-Larix Lakes Loop 8, 84, **86-89**, 90
Rock Isle Lake 8, 86, 87, 88, 89, 90, 94, 95, 96, 97
Rock Isle Lake Viewpoint 86, 87, 88, 91, 93
Rockbound Lake 76, 77, 79

Rockbound Lake trail **76-79**
Rockpile, the 150, 153

Saddleback 120-121, 132, 133, 134, 135, 137
Saddleback trail **132-135**
Sanson, Norman 44
Sanson Peak 44
Saskatchewan Glacier 11, 180, 181, 182
Sawback Range 74
Scarab Lake 103
Sentinel Pass 15, 136, 139, 142, 143, 145
Shadow Lake 108, 110
Shadow Lake Lodge 108, 110
Shadow Lake trail **108-110**
Sheol Mountain 135
Sheol Valley 15, 134, 137
Silver City 79
Silverton Falls 79
Simpson Pass 100, 103
Simpson Pass trail 91, 92
Simpson Valley 87, 88
Simpson Valley Viewpoint 86, 88
Slate Range 157
Snow Dome 184
Spray River 34, 35, 36, 38
Spray River Loop **34-37**, 38, 39
Spray Valley 38, 39
spruce grouse 16
Standish Chairlift 85, 88, 90, 93
Standish Ridge 88, 90, 91, 93
Standish Viewing Deck 88, 90, 93, 94-95
Stella Falls 72, 73
Stewart Canyon 56, 57
Stoney Squaw 60, 62
Stoney Squaw trail **60-62**
Storm Mountain 83, 100, 111, 112, 113
Stutfield, Hugh 177
Sulphur Mountain 42, 44, 48, 60
Sulphur Mountain trail **42-45**
Sundance Canyon 46, 48
Sundance Canyon Picnic Area 46, 48
Sundance Canyon trail **46-49**
Sundance Creek 48
Sunshine Meadows 5, 7, 8, 66-67, 84-85, 86, 87, 96, 99
Sunshine Mountain Lodge 85
Sunshine Road 46, 84
Sunshine Village 84, 86, 88, 90, 92, 96, 99, 100, 103, 107
Sunwapta Pass 180
Surprise Corner 31

Tangle Falls 187
Taylor Creek 117, 119
Taylor Lake 117, 119
Taylor Lake Campground 119
Taylor Lake trail **117-119**

Taylor Pass 119
tea house 9, 120, 128, 129
ticks 16
Tokumm Creek 149
Tower Lake 76, 77
Trans-Canada Highway 4, 5, 18, 20, 21, 53, 56, 60, 63, 67, 85, 104, 117
trekking poles 24
Tunnel Mountain 26-27, 28, 29, 30, 31, 44, 60
Tunnel Mountain Campground 21
Tunnel Mountain Drive 28
Tunnel Mountain Road 31, 32
Tunnel Mountain trail **28-30**
Twin Cairns 90, 91, 92
Twin Cairns-Meadow Park trail 84, 86, 87, 88, **90-95**
Twin Falls 72, 73
Twin Lakes 8, 113
Two Jack Lakeside Campground 22

Upper Bankhead Picnic Area 53
Upper Consolation Lake 153
Upper Falls 72, 73, 74
Upper Hot Springs 42
Upper Minnestimma Lake 142, 143, 145
Upper Twin Lake 113

Valley of the Ten Peaks 143, 146, 149, 151
Vavasour, Nigel 177
Vermilion Lakes 29
Vermilion Pass 83, 111, 114, 116
Victoria Glacier 128, 131
Vista Lake 111

Wapta Glacier 165
Waterfowl Lakes Campground 172
Wawa Ridge 92
Wawa Summit (see *Monarch Viewpoint*)
weather 12-13
Wenkchemna Glacier 146
Wenkchemna Pass 15, 149
Wenkchemna Peak 149
Wenkchemna Peaks 143
Wheeler, Arthur 99
Wilcox Creek Campground 184
Wilcox Pass 11, 154, 184, 185, 186, 187
Wilcox Pass trail 11, **184-187**
Wilcox Peak 184, 187
Wilcox Ridge 187
Wilcox, Walter 136, 146, 147, 164, 165, 187
wildflowers 5, 6, 7, 8, 63, 64, 67, 81, 84, 92, 99, 100, 114, 117, 119, 133, 142, 146, 156, 157, 161, 163, 169, 170, 180, 185
wildlife safety 14-16
Wolverine Creek 104, 105
Wolverine Creek Valley 104

Yoho National Park 5, 149

About the Author

For over 40 years, **BRIAN PATTON** has interpreted the natural and human history of the Canadian Rockies, including stints with CBC Radio, The Banff Centre, the Whyte Museum of the Canadian Rockies, and as a naturalist working for Parks Canada. He has also appeared as an historical interpreter and storyteller in five documentary films about the region. He is also the author of the *Canadian Rockies Trail Guide*, *Parkways of the Canadian Rockies*, *Tales from the Canadian Rockies*, *Mountain Chronicles: Jon Whyte* and *Bear Tales from the Canadian Rockies*. He continues to work on a variety projects from his home in Invermere, British Columbia.